Best,
Love
B.

The
Grandparent
ECONOMY

The Grandparent ECONOMY

How Baby Boomers Are Bridging the Generation Gap

Lori K. Bitter

Paramount Market Publishing, Inc.

Paramount Market Publishing, Inc.
950 Danby Road, Suite 136
Ithaca, NY 14850
www.paramountbooks.com
Voice: 607-275-8100; 888-787-8100 Fax: 607-275-8101

Publisher: James Madden
Editorial Director: Doris Walsh

This publication is designed to provide accurate and authoritative information in regard to the subject matter covered. It is sold with the understanding that the publisher is not engaged in rendering legal, accounting, or other professional services. If legal advice or other expert assistance is required, the services of a competent professional should be sought.

All trademarks are the property of their respective companies.

ISBN 13: 978-1-941688-38-0 | ISBN 10: 1-941688-38-1

Dedication

With profound thanks and love —

To Katherine and Clayton for my history,

To Ashley, Kate and Dwain for my present,

And to Gabriel and Henry, my sweet future.

Today is a grand day for an adventure!

Contents

Introduction

I am uniquely qualified to write a book on grandparents. If you have heard me speak on the mature consumer market you know that my interest in the field of aging began in my childhood. I was raised by my grandparents. Long before I ever read my first report on generational insights, I understood the fundamental differences between my parents' and my grandparents' generations. And I was fascinated.

In the late 1950s and early 1960s, it was unusual for kids to be raised by their grandparents. Divorce was not as prevalent as it is today. When divorce did happen, kids stayed with their mother. Not so in our corner of the Midwest. My parents married very young, went to college, had me, and fell apart. At a very early age, I was on my way to my father's parents' home.

My grandfather was an advertising agency executive and my grandmother an artist and homemaker – heavy influences on my career! My 16-year-old aunt was still in the home. It was a busy, creative household full of colorful people. We returned to the intergenerational lifestyle of pre-war America, where households included older relatives and children all under one roof.

My parents remarried in the early 60s and had my brother. This would be my only venture outside of my grandparents' home. After less than two years, I rebounded to my grandparents, this time with a baby brother in tow. My grandparents were on the verge of retiring from the city to my grandmother's family farm. That's when the real adventure began! My parents stayed on the periphery of my life. My Mom remarried and added two more brothers. I remained close to her parents. My father remarried multiple times, so step brothers and sisters came and went. My aunt divorced and moved home with her daughter. At one point, seven people – four adults and three children – lived in my grandparentsÆ three-bedroom home.

I share this history to make a point. The family issues that drove our reality – mental illness, addiction, affairs and simple immaturity – are the exact same issues that grandparent-led households face today. And there are so many more of these households today, as you will learn later in this book.

Years (and lots of therapy) later I established J. Walter Thompson's mature-focused agency, JWT BOOM, as the pre-eminent advertising agency for companies focused on older consumers. JWT led to the establishment of Continuum Crew, my own firm, focused on mature consumers with a specialization on bringing companies into the digital marketing world. It is here that AARP tapped us to help them understand the grandparent lifestage and its economic power. That research became the genesis for this book.

That same year, I became a grandmother for the first time. Suddenly the research and learning was real! I understood the "bigness" of this lifestage. The idea for this book was initially based only on facts and figures. It evolved into understanding the data in the context of the emotions of grandparenting. I was also asked to partner with the founders of *GRAND Magazine* – the digital magazine for grandparents and their families. Becoming publisher and hearing daily from other grandparents has been wonderful support and an up-close validation of the data.

Of all of the lifestages in later life, grandparenting stands out as the most positive. For many grandparents it is recognition of the continuation of the family long after we are gone. For others, it is the ultimate "do-over;" the opportunity to spend time with grandchildren that we did not have with our children as we built careers. The idea of legacy changes from inheritance-based to experience-based. There is no shortage of emotional content!

As marketers we know that when we touch the heart, it is easier to access the wallet. *The Grandparent Economy* shines a light on the real spending by grandparents on their adult children's families and their grandchildren directly. It also accounts for the time grandparents spend in support of their grandchildren as caregivers, both formally and informally. This spending shifted radically with the economic events of 2008 and changed the dynamics of extended families.

As positive as the lifestage is for the majority of grandparents, there are others who live in uncertainty, balancing their own health and desire to retire with raising their grandchildren – often without their adult children present. Their contribution and needs cannot be under-estimated.

There are thoughtful companies targeting grandparents with products and services based on a deep understanding of their needs and motivations. Any company or organization that targets older adults, or raises funds from older adults, needs to understand the power of the grandparenting lifestage, and the competition for the attention and dollars of this target. There are many product and service categories that are not meeting the needs of today's grandparents, and that's where the opportunity lies.

Thank you for joining me on this journey!

Lori K. Bitter

LORI K. BITTER

Research for
The Grandparent Economy

At The Business of Aging we monitor trends and research in the aging consumer market on a daily basis. For this book, we have combed through the research of respected sources like AARP, Generations United, MetLife Mature Market Institute (which is now defunct), Pew Research Center, Pew Charitable Trust, Yankelovich Monitor, Mintel, Gallup, Nielsen, Blackbaud and Epsilon. We also closely follow the research of Age Wave and the trend reports of JWT Intelligence.

We regularly cut data from the US Census Bureau's reports to add demographic depth to our analysis. Additionally we perform in-depth scans of the grandparent marketplace, including content from experts on topics related to grandparents, their issues and lifestyle. We focus on trends and insights "of the moment," using a proprietary analysis tool to determine the momentum and scope.

Along with experts, we have spoken with hundreds of grandparents. Our relationship with *GRAND Magazine* – the digital magazine for grandparents affords us a unique opportunity to learn first hand what is in the hearts and minds of today's grandparents. We also listen and interact in other online communities and blogs.

To better understand the business implications of the grandparent consumer, we interviewed companies who are successfully focusing on their needs. Likewise, we spoke with non-profits who are involved with grandparents and grandchildren. These interviews, examples, and stories are shared throughout this book.

Finally, we did our own study with an online panel of 1000 grandparents in late 2014. The intent was to fill in the gaps from previous studies and to understand what has changed as the economy rebounds. When we refer to "our study" or "The Business of Aging study," this is the work we are referring to.

The average age of a first-time grandparent has risen from age 48 to age 50. As education levels for women continue to rise and careers advance, women are delaying childbirth. Generation X begins turning 50 in 2015 and are the emerging generation of first-time grandparents

CHAPTER ONE

A Story of Three Generations

Of all of the lifestages common to the middle years of life, grandparenting is the most emotional and positive for mature consumers, and the most financially lucrative for businesses. The shaky economy and the aging of the Baby Boom generation have created an unprecedented consumer market. According to the US Census, there are an estimated 65 million grandparents in the United States alone for a total of 39.8 million grandparent households. With 116.7 million total US households, one in three households in the United States is a grandparent household.

Figure 1

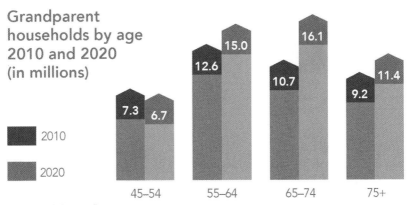

Grandparent
households by age
2010 and 2020
(in millions)

■ 2010
■ 2020

	45–54	55–64	65–74	75+
2010	7.3	12.6	10.7	9.2
2020	6.7	15.0	16.1	11.4

Source: US Census Bureau

For the first time in history we have three distinct generations of grandparents contributing to their grandchildren's lives. Each has unique characteristics based on cohort influences during the formative years of the lives of the members of the generation. "Cohort" refers to a group of consumers born within the same time period, and influenced similarly by events in their formative years their late teens and early twenties as they are forming an identity separate from their parents. Because of these events, the cohort holds a common set of beliefs and perceptions.

Figure 2

A generational perspective

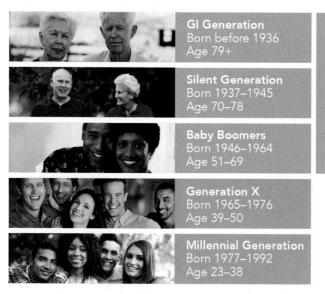

GI Generation
Born before 1936
Age 79+

Silent Generation
Born 1937–1945
Age 70–78

Grandparents

Baby Boomers
Born 1946–1964
Age 51–69

Generation X
Born 1965–1976
Age 39–50

Millennial Generation
Born 1977–1992
Age 23–38

Source: Conventionalized by William Strauss and Neil Howe, *Generations: The History of America's Future, 1584 to 2069*

It is helpful to understand the generational terminology that gets tossed around in the media. The **GI Generation** – sometimes called the Greatest Generation or WWII generation – is now 79+. The **Silent Generation** is a smaller cohort born between the GI generation and the Baby Boom. The **Baby Boomers** represent the current generation sandwiched by the needs of family members younger and older than them. Next are the parenting generations of **Gen Xers**, followed by the **Millennials**.

Figure 3

Cohort influences: Formative years

	WWII	Silent Generation	Leading Boomers	Middle Boomers	Trailing Boomers
Formative Years	1930 to 1945	1946 to 1963	1960 to 1970	1967 to 1977	1974 to 1983
Political/Social	Prohibition, Social Security, FDR/ New Deal, Bread Lines, WWII, Labor Movement	McCarthyism, Cold War, Brown vs. Board, Highways & Suburbanization, Korea	JFK, LBJ, MLK, Civil Rights, Vietnam, Woodstock, Kent State, Draft Lottery	Vietnam, ERA, Watergate, Roe vs. Wade, No Fault Divorce, Casual Sex	Hostage Crisis, Reagan, Terrorism, Middle East Conflict, Rise of Conservatism
Economic	Stock Market Crash, Great Depression, Keynesian Econ	G.I. Bills, Housing Act, Prosperity	New Frontier, Medicare, Great Society	Price Controls, Nixonomics, Inflation	Oil Shocks, Reaganomics, Stagflation
Popular Culture	Chaplin, Babe Ruth, Radio, "Talkies", F Scott Fitzgerald, Movies, Lindbergh, No TV	Sinatra, James Dean, Elvis, Marilyn Monroe, Disney, Hot Rods, Duck & Cover, Sputnik, Family TV	The Beatles, Dylan, Rolling Stone Magazine, Moon Walk, The Pill, Psychedelic Drugs, News TV	Saturday Night Live, All in the Family, Mary Tyler Moore, Ms. Magazine, Counterculture	Star Wars, Disco, Fitness Craze, Punk Rock, Space Shuttle, Crack and Drugs, Crime & Violence TV
Core Traits	Thrifty, Patriotic, Sacrificing, Defer Gratification	Status Quo, "Don't Rock the Boat", Respect Authority	Idealistic, Demanding, Nonconformist, Seek Immediate Gratification	Status conscious, Individualistic, Seek Immediate Gratification	Pragmatic, Apolitical, More Conservative, Fade to Gen X

Source: Age Wave Impact

The WWII Generation lived through the war; they experienced rationing, prohibition and the Great Depression. This resulted in a generation who defers gratification and is thrifty, sacrificing, and patriotic. The Silent Generation is a smaller generational cohort sandwiched between the WWII and Baby Boom generations. This generation was influenced by relative prosperity, integration of schools, the space race and the birth of rock and roll. The Silent Generation is characterized as respecting authority and maintaining the status quo. These older generations of grandparents raised their children and are involved with their grandchildren, but do not meddle in their lives. They saved for their "golden years" after retiring from a job they held most of their lives. Their idea of legacy involves leaving property, large sums of money and insurance proceeds to their family. There is a sense of duty about leaving a tangible inheritance for future generations.

Then came the Baby Boom generation, born into 20 years of unprecedented prosperity in the United States. Post-war optimism and high fertility rates created a huge generation of young people, and a corresponding marketplace of products and services to meet their needs. The suburbs grew to house them, school districts expanded to educate them, companies exploded to meet their "modern" needs: baby food, disposable diapers, baby furniture. Language changed to describe them – teenagers, young adults, and co-eds – as they created lifestages not experienced by previous generations.

John F. Kennedy and civil rights leader, Martin Luther King, politically influenced the oldest Baby Boomers. They experienced Vietnam, Woodstock, and Kent State. While television came into the homes of the Silent Generation, Boomers were the first generation to grow up on television – which famously brought the Vietnam War into America's living rooms. These leading Baby Boomers are idealist and non-conforming. Because the marketplace consistently grew to meet their needs, they are viewed as demanding and needing immediate gratification as consumers.

The Baby Boom spans twenty years. Most experts on the Baby Boom generation argue that there are three distinct cohorts – leading, middle and trailing – and they are so distinct because of the political, economic and cultural influences in their formative years. For our purposes, we look at the Baby Boom as Leading Boomers and Trailing Boomers, as the youngest of the generation fades into Generation X, with a more pragmatic, apolitical view of the world. The Trailing Boomers are the most status conscious, more individualistic, and like their older cohorts, seek immediate gratification. This core trait drove growth of the credit-card industry and deferred payments for all types of purchases.

Boomers parented differently than their parents. They were very involved in their children's schools and activities. This continued into college and career. And now they are just as involved with their grandchildren. Just as they left their mark on every other institution through which they passed, Baby Boomers are changing the face of the grandparent lifestage.

The road back from recession. The economic downturn touched every generation. The oldest generations, already citing high quality healthcare as their number one concern, added "outliving my savings" as an equal concern. Those solely reliant on Social Security benefits feel the most pressure as basic living expenses continue to rise.

The Millennial Generation struggled to launch their adult lives as jobs dried up and older generations held on to their positions longer. Without jobs, many remained in their family homes longer than expected. Older generations, holding on to their senior and management positions, were also blocking Generation X employees from advancement and raises. Every generation experienced the massive lay-offs of the period. Stories abound of older workers, close to retirement, who were suddenly thrown back into the job market competing against younger, less expensive employees.

Businesses struggled to find consumers for their goods and services; it felt as though the entire country had gone white-knuckled into a "spend nothing" bunker. Two key events emerged from this recession. The nature of the family structure and lifestyle had changed. While it was born of "failure" the outcome would be overwhelmingly positive. Second, once all of the marketing noise was stripped away and companies had to get back to the basics, the Baby Boom generation emerged as **the** target with disposable income, need, and new challenges to be met.

Who smashed my sandwich? Prior to the recession, the term "sandwich generation" was used to describe the phenomenon of middle-aged people raising children and caring for elderly loved ones. The stress of this dual caregiving role has been well documented. During the recession and in its aftermath, the squeeze on the Boomer generation has tightened. Seniors hoping to cash in their homes to fund their long-term care could not move. Young people with high education debt could not find jobs and returned home, or required parents' help with expenses while they tried to find jobs.

Boomers lost high-income positions and found it nearly impossible to replace those jobs with comparable positions. Falling back on savings or on a single spouse's income became the norm. Others who were poised for retirement found the needs of their families required them to work much longer in their current roles. This included helping elderly loved ones with contributions of time or money. Boomers, ever optimistic about the future, are forced to admit that their children and grandchildren might not experience "the American dream" and the promise of a better life.

According to a Pew Charitable Trust Report, older Boomers lost 28 percent of their median net worth. Younger Boomers lost more than 25 percent. Middle and lower income Boomers were the hardest hit. They lost more jobs, stayed unemployed longer, and spent down their savings. The bright spot, if you can call it that, is that Boomers are living longer! They are working longer and are channeling their anxiety into correcting their financial outlook. Their elders are also living longer and wish to remain in their own homes. Their children's fortunes are not rebounding as quickly. The "sandwich" is more like a panini pressed in a hot iron grill.

Follow the money. Even in the face of this economic down-turn, people aged 50 and over managed to come out the other side in better shape than younger consumers. According to a

MetLife and Generations United report, 43 percent of grandparents are providing more financial support due to the economic downturn. Thirty-four percent say they are providing financial support even though it is having a negative effect on their own financial security. Every demographic segment says the recession changed their point of view on family relationships, work-life balance, spending, and retirement.

The sheer size of the potential market is compelling for even the most jaded CMO. There are currently over 100 million people over the age of 50.

Figure 4

Population by generation

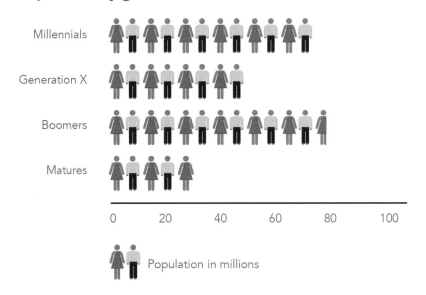

Source: US Census Bureau

There are over 100 million people aged 50+ in the US today. **By 2030, every Baby Boomer will be 65 or older.** Generation X, like the Silent Generation, is caught between two large generational cohorts the Boomers and the Millennials, who are sometimes referred to as "Echo Boomers," and are in fact their children.

With a total US population of approximately 320 million, one in three people is over the age of 50. Further, in the next 15 years, all of the Boomers will cross the 65-year-old threshold. In the next five years, by 2020, the number of Americans 65+ will increase 39 percent. The rate of growth for the population aged 65 to 74 is increasing faster than any other population segment.

Figure 5

Population growth rate by age

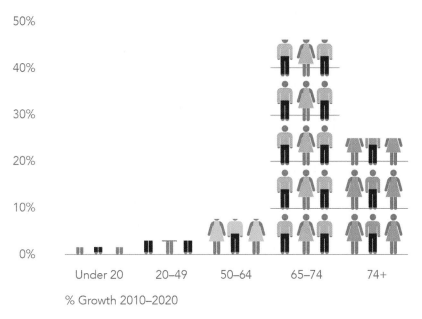

% Growth 2010–2020

Source: US Census Bureau

Seniors are **increasing at a faster rate than younger generations.** This chart looks at change from 2010 to 2020.

The 2013 Consumer Expenditure Report (US Census Bureau) reports $3.2 trillion in annual spending by the 50+ demographic. According to the World Bank, this spending is greater than the gross domestic product of Italy, Russia, United Kingdom,

Brazil and France. Consumers 50+ dominate 119 out of 123 consumer packaged goods categories. Eighty-one percent of the demographic own a home, and 55 percent have no mortgage. The three oldest generations in the United States own 63 percent of US financial assets; when you add assets that Boomers control on behalf of elders and children, that number is closer to 70 percent. In spite of recent economic events, consumer spending in households age 50+ has risen faster than any other age category, outpacing inflation.

Grandparents, as a large segment of the 50+ population, spend. There are nearly 40 million grandparent households in the US, out of a total of 117 million total US households. This means one in three households in the US is a grandparent household. Since 2000, grandparent spending has outpaced general consumer spending, at an average rate of approximately 8 percent annually.

Generational Congestion: Younger, hipper grandparents

Tamar Kasriel of Henley Centre HeadlightVision predicted **a growing sense of agelessness**; people are no longer acting their age, and there is increasing confusion about what behavior is appropriate for different age groups. Former JWT trendspotter Marian Salzman characterized it as "the disappearing generation gap." The majority of today's grandparents are from the Baby Boomer generation; they appear more youthful, vital and active than grandparents of previous generations. Grandparents are spending thousands on rock concerts, hundreds on hip jeans, stocking up on the best anti-aging formulas and scents, while amassing a shoe closet that Carrie Bradshaw would envy.

In a room full of adults over 30, it is becoming increasingly harder to distinguish people by age. Friendships are becoming less generationally focused and are more values and interest driven. In reality the average age of a first time grandparent has been around 48 years, but it has begun to rise in recent years. The median age is 50 for first time grandmothers and 54 for first time grandfathers. This rise in age is driven largely by daughters who are waiting longer to start families – which is closely correlated to higher levels of education and a career focus, plus advances in fertility science, which allow women to bear children later in life.

Still, if you do an image search on grandparents in Google, look at what pops up! You will see photos of people 75 or older in sedentary environments. Or cartoon caricatures of couples

Figure 6

Grandparents by age:
US grandparents percent, by age, 2010

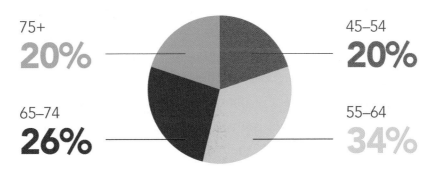

75+
20%

45–54
20%

65–74
26%

55–64
34%

Source: US Census Bureau

In 2010 there were 65 million grandparents in the US. By 2020 there will be 80 million grandparents. **One in three adults** in the US is in the grandparent lifestage.

with gray buns, sagging bellies and boobs, and canes. This is far from the reality of the Baby Boom grandparents. In reality only 20 percent of grandparents are 75 or older.

Stereotypes like this keep companies and organizations from realizing the potential of the grandparent market as a viable target consumer.

Consider the diversity of these famous grandparents – actors Kiefer Sutherland, Jim Carrey, Pierce Brosnan, and Whoopie Goldberg. Musicians Kid Rock, Marie and Donnie Osmond, Sharon and Ozzie Osbourne, Cee Lo Green, and Naomi Judd. Politicians Bill and Hilary Clinton, and George and Laura Bush. Brett Favre holds the title of the only grandfather playing in the NFL. Grey buns? Not a one!

As Figure 6 illustrates the majority of grandparents today are aged 55-74. In 2010 there were 65 million grandparents in the US. By 2020 there will be 80 million grandparents, or one in three adults in the US will be in the grandparenting lifestage.

Educated and Working

Today's grandparents are highly educated and working (75 percent) – very different from generations past. These working Boomers are at the peak of their career earning years and account for 47 percent of the nation's total household income. This work focus drives both time spent with family and the ability to contribute to their children's and grandchildren's futures in terms of time and money. One interesting artifact of more working grandparents is the loss of grandparents as the source of free (or inexpensive) day care when young parents go off to work.

Figure 7

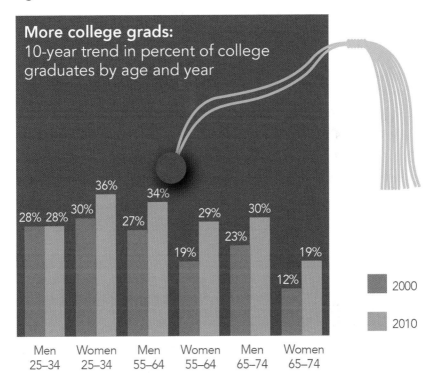

More college grads:
10-year trend in percent of college graduates by age and year

| | 2000 |
| | 2010 |

| Men 25–34 | Women 25–34 | Men 55–64 | Women 55–64 | Men 65–74 | Women 65–74 |

Source: US Census Bureau

More Diverse

This is the first generation of grandparents to signal a shift in the racial and ethnic diversity of the country. The Baby Boom generation represents the first fully acculturated generation of Asians and Hispanics in the US. In fact, approximately 20 percent of today's grandparents are Asian, Hispanic, or African American. This trend continues to grow as younger generations become more diverse.

Baby Boomers mark the first openly Gay and Lesbian population of aging adults. While LGBT people have identified prior to this generation of grandparents, the climate of acceptance plus

Figure 8

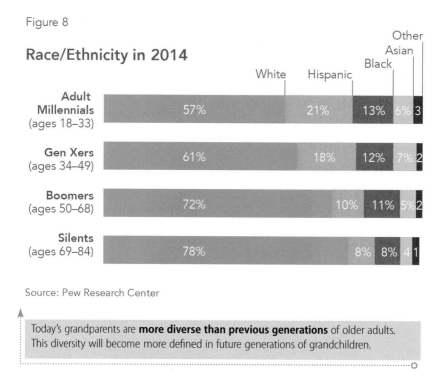

Race/Ethnicity in 2014

Source: Pew Research Center

> Today's grandparents are **more diverse than previous generations** of older adults. This diversity will become more defined in future generations of grandchildren.

the availability of partner benefits and marriage has changed, adding to the diversity of families in the US.

Chopping and Mowing

As mentioned earlier, Boomers parented differently than their parents. Their involvement in their children's lives, schools, and activities was high. Parenting experts called them "helicopter parents" – hovering over their children, and "lawn mower parents" that removed every obstacle from their children's paths. These parents were characterized by waking their college students by phone each morning, addressing professors regarding grades, and even interfering in job and salary negotiations.

I personally experienced this twice in my agency career. First was a father calling to manage his daughter's salary negotiations, making sure I knew about her GPA and the "cost of college to-day." I assured him I understood and that I too had a daughter in college. The second, also a dad, wanted to ask for more paid time off so his daughter could join the entire family for two weeks in Europe. She had only been working for us for nine months. I assured him she was an exceptional employee, but would need to take any additional time as unpaid time off. She was, by the way, mortified that he called me. Imagine for a moment how they will embrace their role as grandparents! Will they meddle with this generation of children in the same way? Or will their over-coddled offspring revolt and force greater accountability on their own children?

Loving Legacy

The idea of legacy is just as strong with this generation of grandparents, as it was with previous generations. In older generations of grandparents this translated to financial gifts, like property, money and other tangible assets being transferred to the next generation. In fact, Boomers will experience the largest transfer of wealth from older generations of parents and grandparents of any generation in history. This may continue from today's grandparents to the next generation, but Boomers appear to be placing greater emphasis on a transfer of values and experiences as their legacy. This is manifesting itself in the desire to share hobbies, do things together as a family, and impart a sense of activism, particularly as it pertains to politics, the greater community, the environmentalism/green movement, and sustainability.

A study by MetLife Mature Market Institute, "Grandparents

Investing in Grandchildren" asked how grandparents want grandchildren to see their legacy. Fifty-two percent said, "I provided for my family even in tough times." Forty-seven percent said, "I taught my grandchildren to make a positive difference in the lives of others."

Figure 9

How grandparents want grandchildren to see their legacy

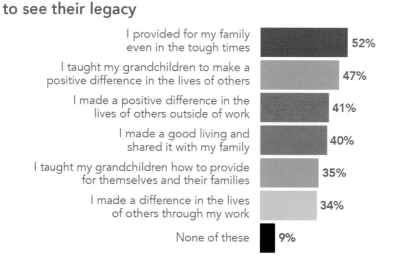

I provided for my family even in the tough times	52%
I taught my grandchildren to make a positive difference in the lives of others	47%
I made a positive difference in the lives of others outside of work	41%
I made a good living and shared it with my family	40%
I taught my grandchildren how to provide for themselves and their families	35%
I made a difference in the lives of others through my work	34%
None of these	9%

Source: MetLife Mature Market Institute and Generations United

Economic Forces

As noted earlier, today's generation of grandparents is educated and working. They plan to work much longer than previous generations. This is the first generation of parents to believe that their children and grandchildren will not be better off economically than they are. The irony is that they may be part of the cause as they hold onto management and C-level positions that their children aspire to. Older women, in particular, are reluctant to leave positions they worked so hard to achieve just as they are reaching their peak years of earning.

While working longer appears to be increasing their peak earning years and enhancing their consumer power, Boomer grandparents are not able to give the gift of time to their children and grandchildren as in generations past. This has implications for day care, summer care, and the comfort level of new moms returning to work from maternity leave. Paid childcare is not an option but a necessity because grandma is still in the workforce.

The MetLife Mature Market Institute and Generations United Report on American Grandparents analysis of Census Bureau data reveals the mean annual income of all grandparent-age households is $68,500 – about $500 above the income of all US households. The same data analyzed for Baby Boomer grandparents reveals a mean household income of $81,000, versus $46,400 for those 65 or older. While this is likely driven by retirement and fixed incomes for those over age 65, 25 percent of all grandparent-age households have an annual income of $90,000 or more. At the opposite end of the spectrum, 25 percent have an income of less than $25,000 per year.

The MetLife and Generations United analysis also indicates that household income for those aged 25 to 44 is declining in real dollars, and so is the availability of entry-level positions. Affluent grandparents will likely contribute to the care and feeding of their grandchildren out of necessity. This may be as simple as clothing or care or as substantial as cars, insurance, and education. In fact, 62 percent of grandparents report providing assistance or monetary gifts over the past five years. The average amount of assistance over that five-year period is over $8,000.

More than half of grandparents report providing up to $5,000 in assistance.

Technology & Entertainment

The availability and acceptance of technology is one of the biggest cultural markers dividing today's grandparents from previous generations. From social media to smartphones to tablets, Boomers have used digital technology in their work lives and, with advances in user experience, have embraced them in their personal lives as well. In The Business of Aging study on digital technology, Boomer grandparents expressed the high value of social media for staying in touch with their grandchildren and keeping up with their day-to-day lives. Grandmothers report learning to text on their smartphones so they can communicate directly with their older grandchildren. FaceTime and Skype are cited as excellent ways to connect when long distance grandparenting.

Grandparents are also funding technology for grandchildren. They report purchasing phones, monthly services, computers, tablets, gaming systems, games, and a multitude of music systems and add-ons. Citing both education and connection as their rationale, the grandparents in our study are willing to pay for more "bells and whistles" than the child's parents. Younger grandparents also believe that technology gives children an advantage in school.

Entertainment is served up on a number of digital devices. While today's grandparents are willing to spend on movies, games, subscriptions, and more in the online world, they exhibit anxiety about the sedentary nature of these activities. They also complain of too much screen time at holidays and family events by adult children and grandchildren. Grandparents seek guidance about "screen time" and how to enhance a grandchild's health and well-being with relevant activities.

True to the generational mythology, Baby Boomers are far more experiential than previous generations. They extend this to gifting for their grandchildren. Ironically they report being strapped for time and having less time to do things with grandchildren than they would like because of their work commitments. On the other hand, they express the desire to provide more experiences for their grandchildren. This ranges from simple activities like fishing, cooking, and reading together, to pricey peak experiences like Space Camp and American Girl adventures. Many cite the need to get grandchildren outdoors and away from technology as a driver for more experiences.

The Family Structure

The nature of the American household structure continues to shift. Multigenerational households are becoming more commonplace. Some of this growth may be due the increased diversity of the nation and cultural expectations of extended family all living under one roof. More often it is due to the economic downturn. Many young-adult parents lost employment and have been unable to find new employment at the same level. Census data from 2010 indicated that there are 4.5 million grandparent-led households with at least one grandchild present. Generations United, an advocacy and resource organization for grandfamilies, report that 7.8 million children are living with grandparents or other relatives. Forty-nine percent had a single parent also in the household. However, 34 percent had neither parent in the household, resulting in 2.7 million grandparents raising young children on their own.

The 2010 Census data also reveals another 2.7 million households where a grandparent is present. Presumably these are older parents living with their adult children. This may be due to finances, healthcare concerns, care arrangements for grandchildren, or cultural expectations. That totals 7.2 million intergenerational households nationwide, and experts believe this number is low.

Kinship care by grandparents continues to grow and is particularly alarming at the lower end of the socioeconomic spectrum, where access to legal assistance, services, and education can exacerbate already fragile household finances. The need for information and advocacy for these grandparents is profound. Generations United's National Center on Grandfamilies works to enact policies and programs to help these families meet their challenges.

Regardless of how or why families are housed together, the research is overwhelming about the benefits to both grandparents and grandchildren. This segment of the population has slightly different needs than traditional grandparents but reports an increased sense of purpose and satisfaction with their lives. This trend may signal a "back to the future" model for families that looks much more like the intergenerational families of the pre-World War II era.

CHAPTER TWO

The Evolving Grandparent

The significance of grandparents today is partially the result of shifting demographics in the past hundred years. Peter Uhlenberg, University of North Carolina, Chapel Hill, wrote in *Historical Forces Shaping Grandparent-Grandchild Relationships: Demography and Beyond:* "Compared to a hundred years ago:

- Children now have more living grandparents.

- More people now have grandparents who live throughout their childhood and into their early adult years.

- Children now have few siblings and cousins to compete with for their grandparents' attention and resources.

- Grandparents now are healthier and have more resources (money and time) to lavish on grandchildren.

- The cultural script for grandparents now is more positive, emphasizing affection and emotional closeness.

- Advances in communication and transportation technology make it easier now to maintain close contact."

Mortality, fertility, and migration have all contributed to the evolution of the grandparent/grandchild relationship. Advances in life expectancy have grown gradually (not the extreme growth sometimes purported) since 1900. Life expectancy at age 65 grew about half a year per decade between 1900 and 2000, which is a very gradual advance. The mortality rate that did make a difference was that of young children. In 1900 fully 25 percent of children did not live to become adults. That number in 2000 was about 1 percent. Also in 1900 about 40 percent of older people would lose an adult daughter before her children matured. That number had declined to 4 percent by 2000.

While the effect of life expectancy has been over-reported, the implications of changes in fertility have been under-expressed. Until 1946, the average number of children per woman declined from 3.6 to 2.1. This changed sharply during the baby boom (1946-1964). In 1957, the peak of the boom, the fertility rate rose to 3.7 children per woman. The boom was not simply a function of more women having children; it was more women having more children.

The Baby Boom put enormous focus on young women of childbearing years. Only 10 percent of those women were childless. But during the same period of time, 27 percent of women over the age of 50 were childless, and never became grandparents. This great divide between older women where more than a quarter had no children or grandchildren, and the grandmothers of the boom is largely an untold story. (Uhlenberg)

When the women who produced the Baby Boom babies reached their mid-grandparenting years (60-64), fewer than 14 percent of women were without grandchildren. In 2020 this percentage for women aged 60 to 64 will rise to more than 20 percent again. Cultural changes – women single by choice, couples childless by choice, and career focused females – all contribute to this trend. (Uhlenberg)

Another outgrowth of the baby boom is the number of grandchildren a set of grandparents had. With three-plus siblings in a 1950's household, grandchildren competed with four sets of cousins for the attention and resources of grandparents. This number – 48 percent – trends downward to 24 percent in 2000. Baby Boomer parents had fewer children. By 2020, 57 percent of young children will have either no cousins or just one set of cousins vying for the attention, time, and resources of their grandparents.

It is also interesting to look at migration, which, in this case, refers to the proximity of grandparent and grandchild. Contrary to headlines, mobility rates have not grown markedly in the last 100 years. According to Census data geographic mobility rates in the 1990s were lower than any decade since the 1950s. The issue of migration is over-stated due to the "snow bird" phenomenon of WWII generation seniors flocking to the Sunbelt to live full-time or for part of the year. Today, as Figure 10 illustrates, nearly 70 percent of grandparents live within 50 miles of their grandchildren.

Figure 10

Percentage of grandparents who have one or more grandchildren by distance

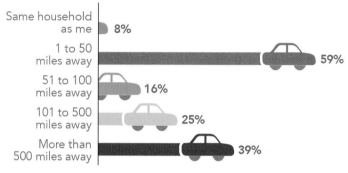

Same household as me ▮ 8%

1 to 50 miles away 59%

51 to 100 miles away 16%

101 to 500 miles away 25%

More than 500 miles away 39%

Source: AARP

The majority of grandparents live **within 50 miles** of their grandchildren.

What *has* changed since the turn of the century is the number of "trigenerational" households. This style of multigenerational living reached its peak around 1900 with about 30 percent of grandparents living with their children and grandchildren. Aging widows made up the majority of these arrangements. Commentators frequently wrote of conflict in these homes and grandparental interference in child rearing.

Images of elderly people as unproductive and superfluous were commonplace as the country became more industrially oriented. The elderly, once valued for their care of small children while their parents worked the farms, saw their value diminished with urbanization and industrialization. By the 1920s, with warnings by "experts" on the issues of co-housing, growing numbers of families pushed for individual households. The Great Depression set this goal back for some, but it was a major outcome of the 1920s. Eventually, Social Security and pensions ushered in an era of prosperity for older people, so grandparents could live independently. Images in media of the time show older people as active and busy, messages that encouraged companionship and loving grandparent relationships.

Finally, the sociology of families had a profound shift. In the 1800s the value of children was often viewed as economic. As soon as they were able, children contributed to the household in some way, particularly in agrarian societies. More healthy children meant more help on the farm. In the first thirty years of the 1900s, children's value shifted to the emotional side of the equation. Similarly, the view of older people in the family changed. Once older people could no longer work – adding economic value – they were seen as a burden to their family. This was not a formula for warm, loving intergenerational relationships.

Over the last century, the nature of the relationship between children and their grandparents has continued to evolve to a more emotionally fulfilling one. As Uhlenberg points out, "A script of grandparents being friends with their grandchildren is quite compatible with the idea of 'successful aging' which involves entering later life as a healthy, active but retired, and economically secure person." He also points out that if this is the sole social contribution of grandparents, it would be of no consequence to greater good!

Today's grandparents have been challenged in the last ten years to provide a greater contribution. The recent recession, beginning around 2006, has had a profound effect on the nature of families and the expectations of a modern household. While the Baby Boom generation lost jobs and had a difficult time finding new employment, and their 401k's were hard hit, they emerged as **the** consumer during this period.

Figure 11

Change 2000–2009 in aggregate household income, by age, 2009 dollars

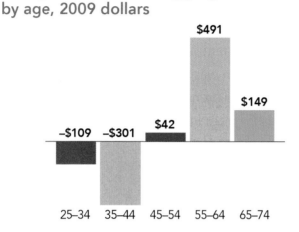

Source: Bureau of Labor Statistics, Census Bureau Current Population Survey

Two times more **workers aged 25-to-34 were unemployed during the recession,** compared with those aged 55-to-64.

Speculation is that the generational optimism of the Boomers drove them to spend their way out of the hole. Regardless of the reason, people over age 50 dominate 119 out of 123 consumer product categories. In fact, only those aged 55 to 64 showed a significant increase in household income from 2000 to 2009. Younger demographics actually lost household dollars.

During this period Baby Boomers were faced with a maze of family issues. Their post-college children could not find jobs, and many finding jobs could not earn enough to live on their own. Rather than subsidize another household, parents needed their young adults to remain at home. This is having a longer-term effect, as it is taking longer for Millennials to establish their own households, career paths, and their own families. Once these children leave home parents report continuing some type of assistance ranging from rent assistance to car payments to phone bills.

Older adults with married children who have young children also stepped up to provide financial assistance. Fifty-two percent of grandparents report providing financial assistance to their adult children. In our research, the presence of grandchildren made older adults twice as likely to provide assistance to their adult children. Emergency help after the loss of a job is the number one category of assistance at 26 percent.

Figure 12

Half of grandparents have provided financial assistance to their adult children

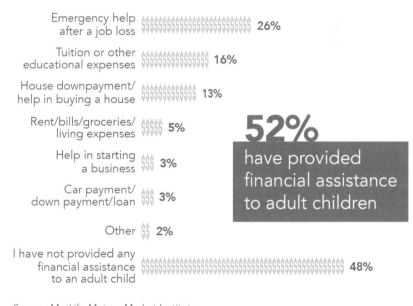

Emergency help after a job loss — 26%

Tuition or other educational expenses — 16%

House downpayment/ help in buying a house — 13%

Rent/bills/groceries/ living expenses — 5%

Help in starting a business — 3%

Car payment/ down payment/loan — 3%

Other — 2%

I have not provided any financial assistance to an adult child — 48%

52% have provided financial assistance to adult children

Source: MetLife Mature Market Institute

The data in Figure 12 from MetLife Mature Market Institute's *The New American Family* report illustrates grandparent support for expenses of daily life, as opposed to luxury items, to spoil their grandchildren – a common stereotype about grandparents.

Caregiving spans the middle years. Most 45-to-65-year-old households provide care for elderly loved ones at some point in time. The years of the recession were no different, but for many families the solutions were tougher. Elderly people on the cusp of requiring assisted living or skilled nursing care could not sell their homes to finance their care in the down market. Boomer children stepped in to help, either helping to pay for necessary care or moving their parents into their homes to provide care.

Some Boomer households reported the triple whammy – college grads who moved back home, young families who moved back home with children in tow to recover from job losses, and an elderly loved one living with them and requiring care. The so-called "sandwich generation" became a stark reality. Though Boomer households fared better financially during the recession, their resources were stretched in many directions.

Relationships could have suffered greatly given the financial and emotional demands. Our research reveals that the majority of families forced into alternative living arrangements considered the experience to be overwhelming positive. Younger adults reported appreciation for their parents and grandparents. They also reported stronger relationships with family overall as a result of being in the home.

The recession aside, the Baby Boom generation of grandparents is different than the previous two generations of grandparents before them. Recall Figure 3 and the Cohort Influences during the formative years of the three generations of grandparents living today. There are fundamental differences in the core traits that resulted from the experiences of their young adult-hood. These are expressed for the WWII generation as thrifty and patriotic, for example and for the Boomers as non-conformist and demanding.

Socio-cultural factors make boomers very distinctive as grandparents. These fall into four categories: Education, Role of Women, Single Life, and Diversity. Baby Boomers are the first generation with open access to higher education. Consequently they have more education than previous generations of older adults. According to the Census Bureau's American Community Survey (2012), 47 percent of adults aged 65 and older have a college education. Fifty-nine percent of adults aged 45 to 64 are college graduates. One result of more education is higher job satisfaction and the desire to work longer – past the traditional retirement age of 65.

The role of women and the family structure changed radically as a result of the women's movement. More women chose higher education over the marriage path. College educated women wanted to work and earn just like their male cohorts. In the era of "having it all" they also had children and returned to work creating an entire industry around dependable care for young children in their pre-school years.

The nature of marriages changed as well. Women became equal partners to their spouses, tipping the male breadwinner model of the 40s and 50s on its head. They had their own bank accounts, retirement savings, and spent independently. Some women became the sole earners in their families while fathers assumed equal or more responsibility for domestic chores and childcare. In professional, two-paycheck households, the standard of living rose appreciably as Boomers entered their years of consumption and accumulating possessions.

The rise in the number of people living solo is also attributed to the women's movement. Educated, earning women no longer needed to be supported in the traditional structure of a marriage. In 1960 there were 7 million single-person households; that number grew four-fold to 31 million single people in 2010. Twenty-seven percent of American households are single-person households. This proportion of the population will continue to rise as young people delay marriage.

Previous generations of older adults were either couples or widows. Fewer than half of all households in 2010 were husband-wife families. The Baby Boom generation has a segment of adults who are single by choice, but many are single as the result of divorce. While divorce rates dropped off during the recession, the rates are trending again at pre-recession rates. Widowhood is still a reality at the oldest end of the age spectrum, with women living longer than men. The gap is beginning to close as Boomer men detect and manage health concerns at a younger age and women's rates of heart disease rise. The predicted outcome of living longer and high divorce rates among older people is that men will age alone for 10 years longer than previous generations and will require care. In previous generations they would have received this from their spouse. Family members, children, and professional caregivers will need to cover these years.

The United States is increasingly more diverse. One in five grandparents is Black, Hispanic, or Asian. The white population stood at about 64 percent in 2010; in the 2015 that share is 62 percent and is projected to be 57 percent by 2025, a total decline of 6.1 percent. The Black and Asian populations will see slight increases over the same period. The Hispanic population, at 16 percent of the total in 2010, will grow 4 percent by 2025 to nearly 21 percent of the US population. The Boomer generation represents the largest and most diverse population of older adults in the history of the United States.

Many Boomer-aged older adults in Hispanic and Asian communities are the first fully acculturated generation in their families. As grandparents, this has tremendous implications on passing down traditions and legacy. Ninety-seven percent believe sharing their heritage is the most important thing they can do with their grandchildren. When raising their children, these Boomers encouraged their kids to be more American and embrace American culture. Now that they are grandparents, they are encouraging their grandchildren to learn about their native cultures and embrace those traditions.

Asian and Hispanic families have a different view of elder caregiving responsibilities. They are also more likely to be living in a multigenerational household, or more likely to consider multigenerational living. Black grandparents are more likely to be raising their grandchildren with or without a parent present, though the grandfamily trend crosses every race, ethnic, and economic line.

No discussion of diversity is complete without looking at older adults in the LGBT community. Within the last five years, openness about sexual orientation has prevailed. Unfortunately, the data has not caught up. According to the American Society on Aging (ASA), accurate estimates of the number of LGBT parents and grandparents are not available. In 2011, the Williams

Institute, using Census data, estimated that there are approximately 9 million LGBT individuals in the US. They also reported same-sex couples were raising approximately 250,000 children under the age of 18 in 1999. They caution that these numbers are conservative estimates and the data are often miscounted. We have found this is particularly true with older LGBT adults who have spent their lives hiding their sexual orientation.

The 2013 American Community Survey attempted to measure same-sex households, both married and unmarried. An abstract on this Census also recounts the issues with counting these households and the under-reporting effect. This report finds 726,600 same sex households in the US. Of those, 26.8 percent are aged 45 to 54; 18 percent are aged 55 to 65; and 15 percent are 65 years and older. This accounts for 60 percent of same-sex households, both married and unmarried.

Data is catching up. This LGBT generation will experience the grandparent lifestage in greater numbers than previous generations. There is an increase in the number of same-sex couples with children, by adoption, artificial insemination, and surrogacy. An understanding of the LGBT grandparent-grandchild dynamic will be important to track over time.

Christine Crosby, who founded *GRAND Magazine* 10 years ago, now publishes the magazine digitally for "today's grandparents and their families." She has observed many differences in grandparenting style as the Boomer generation has stepped into the role. In 2015, she shared some of her insight at American Society on Aging's Aging in America Conference. Even though much attention is placed on the first-time grandparent, with increased longevity, older adults will spend almost half of their adult lives in the grandparenting lifestage.

Figure 13

Grandparenting lifestages
Grandparents at all ages

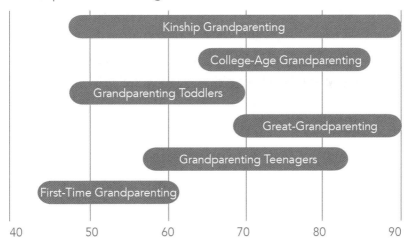

© The Business of Aging

"We have learned so much about grandparents. First, it's not about age; it's a lifestage. Grandparents look younger and have more vitality today. They are motivated. At a time of life when there seems to be so many negatives about the aging process, this lifestage is filled with positive things," says Crosby.

"There are a few key insights we have gained about grandparents today. First, they take better care of themselves so they can be in their grandchildren's lives for a long time. Their own health and wellness becomes important. Second, they are embracing technology and learning new things so they can keep up with their grandchildren and be on the same wavelength," she continues. "We hear a great deal about legacy. Grandparents want to leave a better world for their grandchildren. For many, the birth of a first grandchild is the first time you see life continuing without you! That's a heavy thing to deal with."

"Finally, today's grandparents don't want to wait until they die to create a legacy. They want to create memories with their grandchildren right now. *GRAND Magazine* is full of inspiration on how to do that. From family vacations to backyard projects to reading together, this generation of grandparents wants to be remembered for being there and investing **time** in their grandchild relationships."

To be certain, both grandparents and grandchildren benefit from a strong relationship. Author Susan Pinker wrote in *The Village Effect*, "Children thrive on face to face contact with caring adults. Indeed there is no substitute for such connections when it comes to everything from language through development."

Adults at midlife and beyond tend to experience a powerful desire to nurture the next generation. Older adults who follow this natural impulse to connect with and guide younger generations are three times more likely to be happy in later life than their peers who do not, according to George Vaillant in a Harvard Medical School study. He describes this impulse simply as, "Biology flows downhill."

Many years ago, when the Baby Boomers were still young children, Margaret Mead had this prescription about older adults in the lives of children. "Somehow, we have to get older people back close to growing children if we are to restore a sense of community, a knowledge of the past, and a sense of the future. Nobody has ever before asked the nuclear family to live all by itself in a box the way we do – with no relatives, no support; we've put it [nuclear families] in an impossible situation."

CHAPTER THREE

Understanding Grandparents as Consumers

Older consumers are different. It really is that simple. Consumer behavior is much more difficult to predict as consumers age. This is an issue that confounds younger brand managers and CMOs who move to brands with older consumer markets. They bring all of their marketing genius from their last job and are gob smacked when those strategies for younger consumers do not work.

In the advertising agency business I spent years teaching executives why and how mature consumers respond differently in the marketplace, and how to align their communications for greater effectiveness. Now that the majority of the marketplace is over age 50, it is even more critical to understand the nuances of mature-consumer marketing. It is vital to understanding how to reach the grandparent economy.

This is not a tactical discussion. Tactics are simply a distribution system for messaging. You will not find another discussion of "do they or don't they use digital technology" here. (They do!) What you will find in these next two chapters is a look at why these older consumers respond differently to messaging, without putting you through a graduate course on adult developmental psychology, and a discussion of marketing in the mature-consumer space, as it relates to the grandparent economy. I stand on the shoulders of my mentors in the aging-consumer space. You will see references to our work at Age Wave Impact and the writing of David B. Wolfe.

David's book *Serving the Ageless Market,* published in 1990, is as relevant today as the day it was written. He examines the work of Abraham Maslow and Erik Erikson to help explain the stages or seasons of life and how that affects market behavior. This introduction to adult development coupled with our research at Age Wave Impact, shape my point of view and the market successes my clients have had over the years.

Figure 14

Median age of the resident population of the US from 1960 to 2013

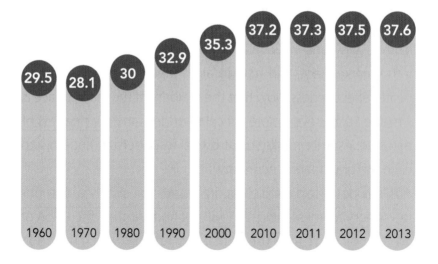

Source: US Census Bureau

Most of our collective knowledge about product positioning and advertising strategy worked when the median age of the United States was much younger – approximately 28 to 30 years of age.

Now that the median age is 40, that thinking must shift. We will look at this more thoroughly in Chapter 4. For now let us look at how and why mature adult "thinking" is different.

It is more correct to say that mature adult thinking evolves. David Wolfe said that human beings are complex, yet we seek oversimplified explanations for our behavior. Honoring that thought we will broadly review the work of adult developmental psychologists.

In *Serving the Ageless Market,* David describes three Experiential Stages of adult life. These three stages reflect the combined sociocultural and psychological influences on an individual moving toward full personality maturation. They are highly complex and intertwined, but are simply described as:

Possession Experience Stage – developing generally in young adulthood; need to establish identity as an adult.

Catered Experience Stage – developing during the middle adult years; enjoying the benefits of full adult identity.

Being Experience Stage – developing around the sixth decade of life; anti-materialistic; when one's fully formed adult identity metamorphoses into a broader human identity.

The *Possession Experience Stage* is experienced in those years when young adults are moving away from their families and establishing their own place in the world. They begin to make choices and purchases that illustrate for the outside world who they are as people. Products are a manifestation of their identity – the clothes they wear, the cars they drive, the smart phone they choose, etc.

The *Catered Experience Stage* occurs in the late thirties through the mid-fifties, depending on the person. At this stage, possessions are taken for granted. The aspirations of the catered experience become more important than the drive for possessions; the novelty of the shiny object is gone. Services that cater to a consumer's needs are king. DIY is out. Having it done for you is in.

Interestingly, this stage coincides with what Erik Erikson, a German-born developmental psychologist and psychoanalyst, described as the "mid-life crisis" years. He was referring to a stage when middle age adults are unsettled with their current psychological and sociological position in life. Adults re-evaluate identity, purpose, and the meaning of one's life. Relationships, careers, and lifestyles may see radical shifts. Things are less important than the issues of life. With more financial resources, middle-aged adults buy experiences that serve this new self. The travel industry reports high volumes of middle-aged people looking for peak travel experiences – adventure travel, cooking tours, and learning tours.

The *Being Experience Stage* begins in the mid fifties and manifests in the sixties for most adults. The "we have arrived" experiences of the Catered Experience Stage shift to confronting the idea of our own mortality. Grandparenting plays a central role in this stage. The birth of a grandchild is frequently the first time older adults think about the family continuing on after they are gone.

The Being Experience Stage is characterized by letting go of regrets, resolution of internal conflicts, and the ability to experience life for what it is. There is a desire for greater connectedness, which enhances the relationship with grandchildren. Acquisition and possessions during this stage are for others or to contribute to personal ideals. It may involve catered experiences. The difference is that the catered experiences are more focused on the aesthetic quality and inner growth.

These Experiential Stages Wolfe described are validated by looking at the work of several noted psychologists. Erik Erikson, mentioned earlier, established eight stages of personality development in his work *The Life Cycle Completed*. Erikson was influenced by Freud. He explored aspects of identity and identified these three: Ego identity (self), Personal identity (what distinguishes one person from another), and Social/Cultural identity (the social roles a person may play).

His theory of development from birth to adulthood considers the impact of external factors, parenting, and society on development of the personality. According to this theory, everyone must go through eight interrelated stages over their life cycle. These eight stages break down by those that are self-oriented and those that are outwardly oriented:

Self-oriented development

1. Infant (Hope) – Basic Trust vs. Mistrust

2. Toddler (Will) – Autonomy vs. Shame

3. Preschooler (Purpose) – Initiative vs. Guilt

4. School Age (Competence) – Industry vs. Inferiority

Up to this point development has been dependent on how a child is treated, or what is done to them. Starting with the Adolescent phase development is dependent on what a person does. This is a phase of discovery, identity seeking, and finding a way to "fit in."

Outward-oriented

5. Adolescent (Fidelity) – Identity vs. Identity Diffusion

6. Young Adult (Love) – Intimacy vs. Isolation

7. Middle-aged Adult (Care) – Generativity vs. Self-absorption

8. Older Adult (Wisdom) – Integrity vs. Despair

According to this theory career and work are paramount at middle age. Responsibility and taking control are significant. Erikson introduced the idea of *generativity* at this stage. Generativity refers to doing something that makes a difference to society. Meaninglessness and doing nothing are fears at this stage. Major life events occur during this period of life, as you will see below in the discussion of lifestages.

The eighth stage, wisdom, involves reflecting on life in a philosophical way. Regret falls away and there is a sense of contentment and fulfillment – a feeling of integrity. Others at this stage struggle with the purpose of life and fear death.

One significant factor in this theory is the movement away from self-orientation with maturity. In marketing terms younger consumers seek self-gratification and older consumers respond altruistically. These stages also support Wolfe's more consumer focused Experiential Stages.

Finally, Abraham Maslow's work helps to explain the contradictions of later life, and also describe the motives that drive development of the person. While most people understand his work as a "hierarchy" with the de facto pyramid of needs, Maslow never used the pyramid. His book, *Motivation and Personality,* provided a theory for understanding human motivation.

Motivations from different levels of the hierarchy can exist at the same time. He recognized that the mind is complex, running parallel processes simultaneously. But certain needs dominate at different times and he focused on the order of meeting these needs. The first four needs are deficit-driven.

- Physiological needs

- Safety and security

- Love and belonging

- Self-esteem and the esteem of others

Maslow originally believed the levels of needs had strict guidelines, but later understood the interrelated nature of levels. Further, he believed that the fifth level of the hierarchy, Self Actualization, could not be achieved without mastery of the other levels.

Self-Actualization is full maturity. It is beyond striving, beyond basic fears. Maslow said, "What a man can be, he must be." It is the realization of one's full potential. Later in life, upon review of the needs, Maslow was most critical of his idea of self-actualization. He extended it to the notion of "self-transcendence." That is, a goal is outside of the self – altruistic and spirit-driven. In Erikson's Life Cycle theory, self-actualization would drive the middle age and older adult stages. The outcome would be integrity and a sense of a life well lived, free from fear and in service of the greater world.

A Model for Understanding the Mature Consumer

The Mature Consumer Influence Model takes a holistic and multi-dimensional view of the consumer. It describes the complex interplay between variables affecting decision-making and how they lead to market behavior for the mature consumer.

Figure 15

Mature consumer influence model

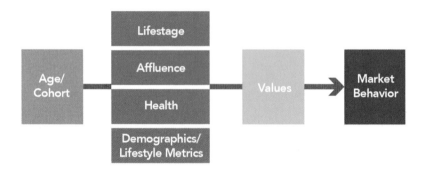

© The Business of Aging

This chart illustrates **a model for understanding the market behavior** of mature consumers. Originally derived from research at Age Wave Impact, the model evolved with the study of adult development and values at J. Walter Thompson's JWT Boom. We continue to refine it as our understanding of the mature consumer evolves.

Age/Cohort is the most fundamental way to understand the mature consumer. We might describe them using the Generational Perspective in Figure 2, or define them by an age range. While age and an understanding of the generational influences of a cohort are important, this is a very esoteric understanding. Unfortunately many of the firms focused on mature consumers stop at this basic understanding.

Demographics and lifestyle metrics are also basic pieces of information, readily available about consumers. These are dimensions that can be easily observed or counted. Like age and cohort, these are descriptive pieces of information – gender, type of dwelling, rural versus urban, etc.

Health status is an important dimension of influence for older adults. It is one of the dimensions that differentiate mature consumers from younger consumers. It is not unusual for older adults to be managing one or more chronic conditions. Differences occur in the management of conditions, access to appropriate care, and lifestyle options that may be contributing factors.

Affluence, a combination of income, investments and access to credit, is a critical dimension in understanding mature consumer behavior and their market motivations.

Lifestage is second only to a person's Values in its importance to buying behavior. Lifestages are life events that occur, sometimes abruptly. A shift into a new lifestage is critically important because it heightens receptivity to new brands, products and services. Consumers shop for and evaluate things that were not previously in the consideration set. They are literally making decisions through a different set of lenses.

Circle back to Maslow's hierarchy.

Figure 16

Maslow's hierarchy of needs

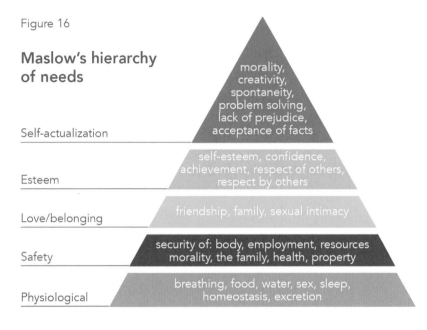

Self-actualization

morality, creativity, spontaneity, problem solving, lack of prejudice, acceptance of facts

Esteem

self-esteem, confidence, achievement, respect of others, respect by others

Love/belonging

friendship, family, sexual intimacy

Safety

security of: body, employment, resources morality, the family, health, property

Physiological

breathing, food, water, sex, sleep, homeostasis, excretion

Source: Wikipedia

Maslow did not believe the need states were a ladder with Self Actualization at the pinnacle, as the pyramid that has come to illustrate his theory shows. He believed any of these needs could be the primary regardless of age or progress through the need states. Consider the effect of divorce later in life. Division of finances and sale of assets can create chaos for the people involved. Esteem falls, relationships are lost. Previously "successful" people are back to needing their safety needs met. Their consumer needs have changed. Choose any one of the lifestage changes shown in Figure 17 and trace it from where people start when a lifestage event occurs and consider the outcome relative to their need states.

Lifestage is not the same as lifestyle. Lifestyle is about what consumers surround themselves with, not taking motivation into account. Lifestage shows us the motivation for a change in the pattern of consumer behavior. Figure 17 illustrates the lifestages experienced at midlife. If you take a moment to consider them, many are about the loss of someone – kids, spouses, elderly loved ones, or something – like a job or career.

Figure 17

Lifestage mosiac

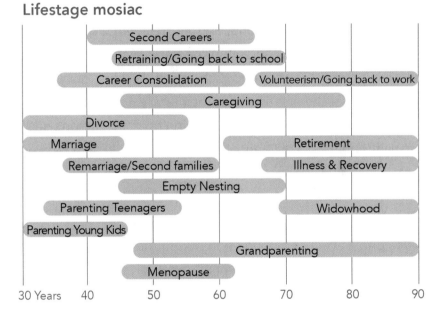

Source: The Business of Aging

Lifestages are life events, sometimes abrupt, that heighten our receptivity to new products and services. We are making decisions through a different set of lenses. This chart illustrates most of the lifestages we experience at midlife. If you take a moment to consider them, many are about the loss of someone – kids, spouses, elderly loved ones. What's important to remember is that **lifestages are dynamic** – we move in and out of them. What matters one day may be completely different the next. We undergo more lifestage changes at midlife than any other point in our lives. If we open this chart up to start in the early 20s – our entré to adulthood – you would see that many more lifestages occur in our midlife than any other time of our lives.

Grandparenting stands out as the most positive lifestage in later life. It is new and exciting, and it is a big consumer moment. Beyond the shopping though, becoming a grandparent is about connection, and sometimes reconnecting on a different level with adult children. Most of all grandparenting is about new love at a time in life when it surprises people. The intensity of watching your child have a child is overwhelming.

For many mature adults, becoming a grandparent fills the need for love and belonging, and also esteem. Especially for Baby Boomers, grandchildren replace status symbols in terms of receiving respect from others. Others see their first grandchild and realize for the first time that their family will continue long after they are gone. It becomes a turning point for Erikson's generativity – making a difference in the greater world as grandparents define their legacy for their children's children.

The Values Funnel

The cohort effect of a generation during the formative years is important and the starting point of understanding mature consumer behavior. It links members of a generation together. But the events or experiences of those years do not have meaning in and of themselves. It is the attitude and belief system formed from those events and experiences that have meaning and create a set of values.

Values act as the "traffic cop" for behavior. They never waver. Attitudes, opinions and beliefs may change. Values are stable. Values are not held as unique or separate ideas. They are part of an integrated system for navigating the world.

The literature on values systems is even more specific. From *Toward a Universal Psychological Structure of Human Values* by Wolfgang Bilsky and Shalom H. Schwartz:

"Values guide actions and judgments across situations; attitudes and opinions, on the other hand are 'domain-specific' (beliefs about a particular object within a particular context). Although attitudes and opinions affect behavior, they are likely to change throughout one's lifetime. Values, on the other hand, are deeply engrained, remarkably stable, and change slowly, if at all, over the course of life. Moreover, values constructs are relatively few in number and are largely universal. Values can be defined as:

a. Relatively stable thoughts or beliefs,

b. About desirable behaviors or ways of living,

c. That transcend situations,

d. Guide decision making, and

e. Are ordered by relative importance."

Nearly twenty years of primary research with aging adults has informed the elements that influence market behavior: age/cohort, lifestage, affluence, health, and demographics/lifestyle metrics. Understanding the relative importance of these on a product or service category, and the value system of the consumer allows us a reliable prediction of market behavior for older adults.

CHAPTER 4

Mature Marketing Today

I have colleagues working in digital and traditional agencies who do great work at marketing to mature adults. At JWT Boom and Continuum Crew we delivered smart, powerful creative on behalf of our clients. Each agency has its own approach for getting there. All of us believe that Maslow was right when he said, "Highly mature adults are less subject to 'enculturation', that is they are more their own person than they were when they were younger." There are idiosyncrasies. David Wolfe told my team once, "They are difficult and puzzling – sometimes contradictory – but there is always a reason!"

You can only know that reason by knowing the consumer. In my career I have been involved in over 100 studies on older adults and product categories relevant to them. That is a lot of research! I have probably read every relevant study on this market by the other leaders in this space. Many of them are quoted in this book. Recently, with the availability of online survey tools and inexpensive methods for data collection, I have seen some really poor research. This is not the fault of the tools. Frequently in a rush to get information from the market (typically to show potential investors) companies ask questions that have already been asked (usually in a better way), or ask questions that are leading the consumer to their own point of view. The result is a set of statistics with no real insights. Statistics don't buy things. People do. Don't get me wrong, surveys are very important; but so is actually talking to older consumers. In our technology-driven agency environments I find that no one wants to actually talk to anyone!

Even the agencies that "specialize" in mature consumers do some pretty bad research – usually for the PR value or to garner more speaking engagements. Most of it has been done before. Better. Nearly every product category relevant to older consumers has a deep history of research. A survey of all of the existing research and literature, which takes time, will tell you what has been asked and answered. It will also tell you where the white space is for new inquiry. Reading the questionnaires created by respected research organizations will help you understand the best way to phrase a question, and also the types of questions to use for particular information.

The best research insights and outcomes for our clients always start with talking to consumers to understand more about their relationship to the product, service, and category. This line of inquiry is based on our survey of all of the existing literature and research; don't waste precious research time and dollars asking what has been asked before. Depending on the goals of a project, we might stop at this phase. Most often, this learning informs the creation of the survey work and becomes part of our final report. Increasingly, we go back to consumers after the survey to probe the findings, gain more insight, and understand more about the road to purchase.

I share our experience because there is complexity in understanding the reasons why older adults do what they do. Our work with grandparents especially illustrates this. Follow this example: Zoe is 14, turning 15 this month. Her mom knows she wants the new iPhone. She has been waiting until Zoe is 15 to let her have a phone. Unfortunately, mom has not been able to find full-time employment, though her part-time job has potential if she just hangs on for a bit longer. Her husband has a good job, but with three kids, things are tight. Just having a birthday party is a stretch right now.

Mom's parents Andrea and Steve live several neighborhoods away and are particularly close to Zoe, their oldest grandchild. They have paid for her gymnastics classes since she was four and often pay for fees and costumes for competitions. They also have a 529 college savings plan for her and her two younger brothers. They have been asking Zoe's mom for birthday gift ideas. Mom explains the financial dilemma to Andrea and her reasons for wanting Zoe to have a phone. Andrea agrees that Zoe is mature enough for the responsibility. Andrea and Steve discuss the phone and the fees and check with their cell carrier to see what type of plan they could get that would include Zoe. They were excited to learn that the phone is half-price with a two-year contract, and they can add Zoe to their plan for additional $10 per month. The phone is purchased and Zoe is thrilled on her birthday.

This is a complex purchase path. Zoe is the end-user; Mom is an influencer; Andrea and Steve are the purchasers. We see the same level of complexity with caregivers who are providing care for elderly loved ones. A survey does not capture these nuances, but talking with consumers does. The multigenerational nature of today's lifestyles demands that we do our homework. Many of the mistakes we see in business plans for older adults happen when the company doesn't know what they don't know.

Companies right now are asking for counsel on how to target both the Boomers and the Millennials simultaneously. Increasingly, both generations are involved in the category of considered purchases. Millennials may identify a need and show preference, but the Boomer parent is an influencer and often the purchaser. We have seen this in categories ranging from personal luxury goods to first homes.

Why Advertising Has Stopped Working

I studied advertising and marketing in graduate school. I learned about the founding fathers of the business and the creative geniuses that shape the way we think about great advertising today. My grandfather was in the agency business. So was my father. I have two daughters who followed me into the business. Not much has changed. Seriously. Media has certainly changed. Measurement and metrics have evolved. The jargon is ever changing. But the basic tenets of creating great advertising really have not changed. It starts with these pure insights about the consumer.

The link between research and creative work, the Planner/Strategist, has been all but eliminated in many agencies. Frequently we hear that the salary was moved to fund analysts to go through the data being collected, social media specialists, and digital producers. All of these roles are important, but not at the expense of the Planner/Strategist. Many agencies claim everyone on the team is charged with strategy (true enough) or the role is part of the work of the account team or the creative team. The account team champions the client point of view. The creatives own the ideas. Without the clear voice of the consumer, relevancy is lost. The Planner/Strategist knows the research and has mined it for those insights that will be most meaningful.

This role is critical when the target is an older consumer. Besides understanding the cohort influences and the lifestages of consumers over age 50, the Planner/Strategist has to grasp the subtleties of the psychology of older adults. For example, adult development psychologists have noted psychological changes that occur in both men and women, typically in their 50s. In contrast to younger men, older men show less interest in the role of conqueror, or power grabs. They show a higher interest in loving relationships and giving to those relationships. Conversely, across a broad range of cultures, women move psychologically in the other direction. In *The Pathfinders* Gail Sheehy writes, "Even in normal patriarchal societies, women become more aggressive in later life, less affiliated and more managerial or political."

In short, men move toward more "female" qualities and women move toward more "male" qualities. This is often attributed to shifting hormone levels in the middle years, and explains the sense of calm or balance some couples experience in their middle years. Regardless, it is important to know when creating messages that resonate with older adults.

The concept of 360 degree marketing and CRM in today's

terms works for today's CMOs because the algorithms account for all that can be measured the data of the consumer. But it fails to account for biological or psychological factors that shape consumer behavior. When those factors are disregarded, there can be no understanding of mature consumers.

The "Unchanging Man"

David Wolfe once reminded me of a story about Bill Bernbach, one of the true geniuses of the advertising business. Famous for the introduction of the VW Beetle into the US and the founding of Doyle Dane Bernbach, he once said, "I warn you against believing that advertising is science." On his death in 1982, *Harpers* magazine described him as having "a greater impact on American culture than any of the distinguished writers and artists who have appeared in the pages of *Harpers* during the past 133 years."

Bernbach's work is fresh, human and empathetic, making the campaigns he crafted near perfection. He is quoted as saying, "Human nature hasn't changed for a billion years. It won't even change in the next billion years. Only the superficial things have changed. It is fashionable to talk about the *changing man*. A communicator must be concerned with the *unchanging man* – what compulsions drive him, what instincts dominate his every action, even though his language too often camouflages what really motivates him."

Wolfe, in *Ageless Marketing,* challenged us as marketers in the mature consumer arena to learn to "tap the soul of the unchanging man." To do that requires insight and an understanding of the archetypes, root motivations, and powerful emotions that consumers may not realize are lurking beneath the surface. Has an ad ever brought a tear to your eye? Recall the ads that Hallmark used around the Hallmark Hall of Fame productions. Or the McDonald's ad featuring a retiree going to his first day of work. Fast forward to the recent ads by the National Association of Realtors about the "American Dream of home ownership" featuring a grandfather and his grandson. Mature consumers appreciate the art of a story well told. Brand stories are memorable, years later.

The "unchanging man" is what makes talking to older consumers so critical. Understanding what lurks beneath the stereotypes of Boomers and seniors is the insight that creates great advertising that sells products and services.

"The Battle for Your Mind" Has Evolved

The 20th Anniversary Edition of *Positioning: The Battle for Your Mind* was released in 2001, introducing the fundamentals of product centric positioning to a new generation. Al Ries and Jack Trout, the authors, created a blueprint for absolute positioning, or the act of fixing a brand in the mind of the consumer on a mass basis.

They wrote, "It is quite difficult to change a consumer's impression once it is formed. Consumers cope with information overload by oversimplifying and are likely to shut out anything inconsistent with their knowledge and experience. In an over-communicated environment, the advertiser should present a simplified message and make that message consistent with what the consumer already believes by focusing on the perceptions of the consumer rather than on the reality of the product."

The Baby Boom generation was the young adult market when Ries and Trout developed this approach to fixing a brand in the minds of mass consumer market. The concept continues to hold up for young adults. But it ceases to work effectively to position brands for older adult markets.

Older consumers have become so individuated that absolute positioning is difficult. They are more resistant to being told what is and what is not. Their own (and their cohort's) experience as a consumer is more trusted. Mature consumers believe they are capable of their own choices and will bring their own meaning and value to a brand.

Conditional positioning is more effective. It is about the consumer and not the product; it encourages a person to define a brand from their own unique point of view, filtered through their values, worldview, needs, and behaviors. While absolute positioning is about what the brand brings to the party, conditional positioning is about what the consumer brings. There is a more nuanced relationship with a brand and a comfort with ambiguity that aligns more effectively with the psychology of the older mind.

Harley Davidson is a great example of a brand that is conditionally positioned. It engages the rebel in everyone – whether you are a regular in a biker bar, a lawyer who rides on weekends, or a woman who always wanted to ride. The brand has broad appeal. When you leave room for consumers to bring their hearts, minds and imaginations to the brand, you get a much deeper level of engagement with the brand. I have a nephew-in-law named Harley for his dad's love of the brand. Harley Davidson's annual report has this to say about brand loyalty, "Retention is for wimps. We measure the percentage of customers who have our name tattooed on one of their body parts." That is commitment!

Saatchi & Saatchi created a modern twist on positioning with *Lovemarks: the Future Beyond Brands.* "Brands have run out of juice. People expect great performance from products and services," they report. "Lovemarks transcend brands. They deliver beyond expectation. They sit on high levels of respect. Lovemarks reach your heart, as well as your mind, creating an intimate, emotional connection that you can't live without. Lovemarks inspire 'loyalty beyond reason.'"

Brands haven't run out of charisma. The mass of the consumer market has matured, forcing the brand relationship to move from the left-brain with its logical, absolute position to the intuitive, philosophical right brain. The intangibles of Lovemarks are three elements: Mystery, Sensuality, and Intimacy. Take a look at these descriptions:

Mystery draws together stories, metaphors, dreams, and symbols. The past, present and future become one. It is about what's left to learn and wonder at.

Sensuality keeps the senses on alert. Think textures, scents, tastes, and music; how we experience the world and create memories.

Intimacy refers to empathy, commitment, and passion. Without conviction there can be no love.

Not surprisingly, these are all elements that require the consumer to bring something of themselves to the brand relationship: a conditional positioning that is exactly what the mature consumer expects from a brand.

The brands that reach Lovemark status are age-ambivalent. They resonate across a broad range of consumers regardless of their demographic designation. Older consumers can relate to them, and younger consumers feel aspirational towards them, which brings us to David Wolfe's concept of agelessness.

In *Serving the Ageless Market – Strategies for Selling to the Fifty-Plus Market,* Wolfe wrote, "When I use the term Ageless Market, I am referring to those members of maturity markets for whom age has ceased to be a major factor in self-definition, lifestyles and attitudes, by virtue of their having substantially achieved full maturity. While this phenomenon may occur earlier, it generally manifests itself in mature individuals sometime during their sixties, when a person begins to grow in Erickson's eighth stage, the stage of wisdom."

Contrary to the stereotypes of the Boomer generation, this is not denial of aging or yearning for lost youth. It is a more centered sense of the timelessness of all things. In his subsequent book, *Ageless Marketing,* Wolfe proposed that agency creatives lean into ageless marketing that is inclusive of everyone, without regard to age. It was a path we followed at JWT Boom, believing that ageless marketing is like universal design. When you design for the oldest part of the population, you create a better environment for people of all ages. The majority of Lovemarks live in this space.

Marketing to Grandparents

Though Maslow never intended to be a marketer, when it comes to creating products, services, and messaging for older adults, his "13 personality attributes of the self-actualizing person" from *Toward a Psychology of Being* provide focused guidelines for creating a great brief. Recall that self-actualization is the realization of one's full potential, with a focus outside of self. Many of the grandparents we spoke with considered this phase of their development to have begun with the birth of that first grandchild. It is described as a turning point, as a time when the future comes into sharper focus. There is a realization of their mortality, and of family life continuing after they are gone. Relationships take on greater meaning and a sense of selflessness takes over.

Here are Maslow's attributes, with notes on how they relate to communicating with grandparents. A self-actualized individual has:

1. **Superior perception of reality.** Mature adults see things that younger consumers cannot see. Advertising claims are met with a much more discerning eye, and a world of consumer experience.

   Grandparents are particularly perceptive about communications that ring false in terms of what real families look like, unrealistic family situations, and lifestyles in advertising.

2. **Increased acceptance of self, others and nature.** They are more mellow, contrary to the stereotype of the hyper-focused Boomer. They appreciate a smart sense of humor.

   For grandparents, there is a sense of greater enjoyment

of their grandchildren versus their own children. They are more relaxed and present than they were as parents. Grandfathers, in particular, observe this, saying they were busy working when their children were small, so they have a "do-over" with their grandchildren.

3. **Increased spontaneity.** There is a sense of the importance of each day, and being present.

    While parents are more focused on schedules and planning, grandparents can be more spontaneous with their grandchildren with a "seize the moment" approach.

4. **Increase in problem-centering.** There is a focus on problems beyond themselves; they are mission-oriented on responsibility and obligation.

    Grandparents report that they have an increased desire to leave the world a better place for this future generation of grandchildren. They volunteer, give to charitable causes and support organizations and principles with this mission.

5. **Increased detachment and desire for privacy.** This does not mean an older adult is solitary. There is a high sense of security and comfort with time spent alone. This stage of life is highly reflective.

    For many grandparents this corresponds with their grandchildren's tween and teen years. Grandparents report their broader perspective on their own history provides them with perspective to guide their grandchildren through tough situations, which they are often reluctant to share with their parents.

6. **Increased autonomy and resistance to enculturation.** Older consumers know their own mind and what they want and expect from brands. They are not dependent on external forces for cues about the relative importance of these things.

   As grandparents, they extend this value to children. It is expressed in situations when children need to overcome peer pressure, bullying, and for older teens, issues with drugs, alcohol, and sex. As mentioned above, teens frequently turn to grandparents as non-judgmental versions of their parents for advice in these situations.

7. **Greater freshness of appreciation and richness of emotional reaction.** Mature people experience a sense of wonder and awe in the everyday experiences of life.

   First-time grandparents embody this. Without the sleep deprivation and stress of becoming a parent, grandparents find pure joy in every event in a new baby's life. They report a change in the relationship with their adult child as well.

8. **Higher frequency of peak experiences.** Peak experiences open up feelings of wonder and the idea of limitlessness. The experiences, and the resulting feelings, carry over into daily life and create meaning.

   Grandparents from the Baby Boom generation express the desire to share experiences with their grandchildren throughout their childhood as opposed to the legacy of cash or real estate, which is more prevalent with older generations. These are not necessarily expensive experiences and include things like learning to cook, using tools, and fishing, in addition to family vacations.

9. **Increased identification with the human species.** Older people at this phase of life exhibit more compassion, empathy, and sympathy for others. This manifests itself with the desire to do more for others.

   Like the generations of seniors before them, Baby Boomers give to charitable organizations and volunteer in their communities. Grandparents report being especially responsive to organizations focused on children and their needs, both in their community and in the greater world at large.

10. **Improved interpersonal relations**. The circle of friendships tends to become smaller and more intense. These are relationships for their own sake, not for what friends do for you socially or otherwise. Many people at this stage find that people with like values are attracted to them.

    Grandparents who are geographically close to their adult children report that the falling away of esoteric friendships tends to happen with the birth of their first grandchild. Family relationships take precedence and only the closest of friendships are maintained.

11. **More democratic character structure.** Actualized mature adults have a sense of fairness and humility. There is no discrimination about class, education, race, or color.

    Grandparents report a number of teachable moments at different ages and stages of their grandchildren's lives. They express concern over discrimination at every level and believe it is part of their job as grandparents to create good citizens of the world.

12. Greatly increased creativity. The shift from left brain – *rational* – to the right brain – *creative* – opens a window of creative possibility. Without the judgment of others in the picture, older adults can invoke their inner poet and philosopher.

While grandparents sense this movement toward their own creativity as they age, they are also more likely than parents to recognize the need for creative outlets for their grandchildren. While parents may be more academically and sports focused, grandparents have a broader view. They are also likely to pay for lessons, events, and opportunities for creative expression – more so than sporting.

13. Certain changes in the value system. Older consumers values systems do not radically reform, but their sense of priorities shift. Being ethical is highly valued.

Boomer grandparents express that their idea of what is right has changed. While in their younger parenting years they may have taken a "the end justifies the means" approach, they now believe it is their obligation to help teach ethical lessons. This involves sharing their stories openly with their children and grandchildren.

Several other key themes evolved from our grandparent research that are important to communicating with people in this life stage. The Baby Boomer generation of older adults does not find meaning in leisure. Messages about abundant free time in retirement do not resonate. Leisure time is about family and re-connecting with self, not an end of its own. Older adults crave purpose in their later years.

Purpose also relates to work and retirement. Many Boomers report delaying retirement because work gives them a sense of purpose and accomplishment. Like it or not, in our society you are what you do. Loss of structured work frequently equals loss of purpose. In fact, suicide rates among adult males over age 65 are four times the rate of younger men. Gerontological psychologists attribute this high rate to the devastating loss of purpose that can result from the absence of productive work to validate one's existence. More Boomer pre-retirees report having detailed plans for work, travel, and volunteerism before their actual retirement in order to make the transition more personally fulfilling.

In *Vital Involvement in Old Age,* Erick Erikson, Joan Erickson, and Helen Kivnic speak of the need for purpose among older adults. "The vital involvement of which they speak is not the kind of playtime involvement widely seen in advertisements for travel, housing and other products and services. It is involvement that results in some product of effort perceived by others as having value. *Contributions of value* are vital to one's sense of well-being, hence the term *vital involvement.*"

For the majority of adults in our study, being a grandparent is the number one response for what is providing a sense of purpose at this stage of life. They mention the ability to teach and mentor as very important. The idea of a parenting "do over" also scores as very important.

A second theme that emerged is the feeling boomer

grandparents have about the stereotypes of the Baby Boom generation. The images of self-entitled, self-centered, and materialistic boomers do not sit well, and the majority of those surveyed believe advertisers and reporters frequently get it wrong. From a developmental perspective self-involvement and materialism are features of a striving lifestyle typical of younger adults, which would be accurate for any generation, not just the Baby Boom.

Third, our survey looked at purchase behavior. We examined a number of theories about mature adult behavior and the grandparent lifestage. Because of the recent fluctuations in the economy, understanding price and value was important. Price was a more important factor in the choice of basic items; quality and brand names was the primary factor. For more discretionary purchases they showed less price sensitivity. This was particularly true if the outcome or experience derived from the item or service had greater value. Consistent with adult developmental psychology, experience trumps price! There is willingness to "bargain shop" for a regular set of basic items in order to afford more experiential purchases. This includes the use of coupons, special offers, or loyalty programs.

In interviews about purchase behavior, there was a strong pattern of decision behavior for more expensive, experiential products and services. The majority of consumers reported making "gut" decisions based on their experience or intuition. But following that decision they created a list of reasons to validate the decision. In other words, the purchase of highly valued products starts in the emotional right brain, and then is rationally supported by the more logical left brain. Communication must connect with grandparents on an emotional level first, and then provide post purchase support points for their decisions.

Finally, campaigns and promotions that invoke a false sense of urgency fall flat with mature consumers. Experience in the marketplace is certainly one reason. They understand the cycle of sales and promotions, or have a perception that sales or bargains happen frequently, so any sense of urgency is overstated. More important is the feeling that they are in control of the timing of the purchase and will make it when it is right for them.

CHAPTER FIVE

Grandparents:
The Three-legged Stool

Not every grandparenting situation is ideal. At *GRAND Magazine* we talk about the grandparenting lifestage as the "three-legged stool." **The first leg** is the world of everyday grandparents who experience the joy of grandparenting in a very conventional way. **The second leg** is grandfamilies. There are grandparents raising their grandchildren and dealing with the unique set of issues of having children in your home during the later years of life. **The third leg** of the stool is grandparents who are alienated from their grandchildren.

Youth Caregivers are an important sub-segment of grand-families, as these children are providing daily care for parents and grandparents so they can continue to age at home. Blended families – families created out of divorce and remarriage – are also an important segment of the grandparent market.

Grandfamilies

Grandfamilies, also known as kinship families, are families where children live with and are being raised by their grandparents or other members of the extended family. Today, 7.8 million children live in grandfamilies, where grandparents or other relatives are the head of the household. One in ten grandparents live with their grandchildren. Of those, 4.9 million grandparents are the head of the household. Grandparents save taxpayers $4 billion each year by raising their grandchildren and keeping them out of the foster care system.

Of the 4.9 million grandparent households, 2.7 million of those have no parent present, so the grandparents provide the sole means of support for their grandchildren. Contrary to the stereotype of this being a "poor people" problem, grandfamilies live in every area of the country and represent all income levels, races, and ethnicities. Still 25 percent of children living with grandparents are living in poverty. Fifty-eight percent of these grandparents are still in the workforce and 40 percent of them have been providing care for more than five years.

"Grandparents often take on the care of grandchildren with little or no chance to plan in advance. As a result, they face some pretty unique circumstances," said Donna Butts, Executive Director of Generations United. "This isn't something new. George and Martha Washington raised grandchildren at Mount Vernon. Today's grandfamilies are diverse. We've had three wars with extended deployment, so grandparents stepped up. Demographics are changing. We had job losses during the recession so young families moved in with grandparents, and some left their children to find work. Divorce, deportation, substance abuse, incarceration, mental illness all contribute to the issues."

Generations United is a 30-year-old not-for-profit organization whose mission is to improve the lives of children, youth, and older adults through intergenerational collaboration, public policy, and programs. Generations United houses the National Center on Grandfamilies, the leading voice for advocacy and support for these families.

One of the biggest issues grandfamilies face is a lack of legal standing for simple things like school enrollment and healthcare needs. Butts reports that frequently a senior-living situation does not accommodate children – legally or in terms of space and need. Because these caregiving grandparents are in their prime years for retirement savings, money often gets funneled to care for their grandchildren, so their own retirement is at risk. Grandparents who are already retired may not have the extra resources for raising children.

In spite of all of the challenges that grandfamilies face, children do well in the care of grandparents. Compared with the option of foster care, they report being more stable, more connected to their siblings and to their communities. "There are very positive things about living together, it's not always the case that something is 'wrong' if you live together," said Butts. "There is frequently caregiving going on at both ends of the spectrum, with grandchildren helping their grandparents as well. There can be financial benefits to having a larger home with everyone together under one roof. It can make families stronger. We also know that these children have closer grandparent relationships and grandparents are passing on their culture, traditions and providing roots for these grandchildren."

Today's grandfamilies need a voice, especially on issues of

immigration and child welfare law. Many communities have created "kinship navigators" to help grandparents find information about school enrollment, financial assistance and medical care all in one place. Generations United, the American Bar Association Center on Children and the Law, and Casey Family Programs, support Grandfamilies.org.

● ● ● ● ● ● ● ● ● ● ● ● ● ● ● ● ● ● ●

Addiction and Grandfamilies

A recent story in *The Boston Globe* highlights the number one reason today's grandparents cite for taking over care of their grandchildren – addiction. In an article titled, "Opioid addiction among parents leads to more grandparents raising grandchildren," Katheleen Conti reports that in Massachusetts "80 percent of people raising their children's children had custody as a result of substance abuse issues."

Grandparents are stressed by the dual pressures of raising grandchildren and the constant worry for their addicted children. It is isolating and stressful. Many have had to cut back on work to provide care because the cost of childcare is prohibitive, and foster care is unthinkable. It is emotionally and physically exhausting.

"Often grandparents have to grapple with devastating choices, such as being forced to move out of their senior housing program because facilities don't allow live-in children, or putting the grandchild in foster care because health or financial barriers prevent them from taking custody," writes Conti.

Grandparents are frequently dealing with infants born addicted, with their own health problems, plus adult children in rehab programs who hope to reclaim their role as parents. They remain hopeful that their children can resume parenting in a clean environment so that they can step back into their role as grandparent.

Grandparent Alienation

Alienated grandparents have been cut off from contact with their grandchildren. Frequently this abandonment occurs following a divorce and change in custody for the children, or in the case of parents who never married. Sometimes remarriage and re-formation of family structures can be an alienating force. Often this alienation occurs when the parent-child relationship was not healthy to begin with. Parents become grandparents and expect to get a "do over." Adult children are not so receptive. Issues with boundaries, religion, and unhealthy habits like drinking and smoking are cited.

Grandparents are embarrassed to talk about this issue, often saying they do not know what they did to cause the separation from their grandchildren. It is a very common issue that crosses all socio-economic lines. Grandparents experiencing this loss are wounded emotionally and psychologically by their adult children. Many grandparents in this situation are organized through organizations like Alienated Grandparents Anonymous (AGA).

AGA believes, "Alienation is a willful intimidation. It involves such issues as personality disorders including narcissistic personality disorder, borderline personality disorder, delusional disorder, etc.; unresolved childhood issues; pathological lying; brainwashing; mind control; neuro-linguistic programming; and cult-like thinking. It is about power and control." Alienation creates emotional issues and confusion for children, and is considered by experts to be a severe form of child abuse and elder abuse.

Though no clear statistics on this issue are available, experts believe it affects millions of grandparents. In our research every person interviewed knew a grandparent affected by this type of abandonment. In the majority of cases in our study these are parents of sons who did not marry their child's mother, are divorced, or have issues with a problem daughter-in-law. Regardless, grandparents are devastated by the decision to separate them from their grandchildren.

There is a movement to establish Grandparent Rights for visitation with children. State statutes vary, and the goal is a uniform law for each of the United States. The Supreme Court in *Troxel v. Granville* struck down a statute in Washington State about third parties seeking visitation with children. It was considered overly broad and interfering with a parent's right to make decisions for their children. Laws are being constantly revisited.

Alienated Grandparents Anonymous (AGA) focuses on the struggle many grandparents have in being part of their grandchildren's lives. AGA provides support and information, and helps validate the feelings of those suffering some degree of estrangement, alienation, or isolation. The goal is bringing alienated grandparents, parents, and grandchildren together.

Hidden Family Heroes: Caregiving Youth

Not every multigenerational household is the story of happy grandparents supporting loving parents in their effort to raise successful grandchildren. Caregiving is the number one reason for multiple generations to be residing together, and creates a complex set of family dynamics. When the caregiver is a child caring for a parent or grandparent, there are multiple issues of concern.

The only data of a decade ago, revealed there were approximately 1.4 million children (conservatively) in the US who provide care for family members who cannot manage their own care without assistance. More than 3 percent of households with a child from 8 to 18 years of age, include a child caregiver. Thirty-one percent of these children are ages 8 to 11, and 38 percent are ages 12 to 15. These young caregivers are more likely to live in lower-income households with a single parent.

Seventy-two percent of these children are caring for a parent or grandparent or even great-grandparent, and they are helping with activities like bathing, dressing, feeding, and toileting their loved ones, in addition to shopping and making meals. In short, they are doing everything that adult caregivers do but they still have school and activities in addition to their caregiving role and have no recognition or benefits offered to adult caregivers.

Connie Siskowski, RN, PhD, founded the American Association of Caregiving Youth (AACY) in Palm Beach County, Florida, to shine a light on the existence and issues of these children, and to find ways to support their unique needs. Connie's childhood experience as a caregiver for her grandfather shaped her passion for this work. In her county alone, more than 10,000 middle and high school students are involved in family caregiving.

According to Siskowski, "At a time when children are still developing physically and emotionally as well as needing to achieve academic success, their lives become consumed with worries about their family so their stresses build. Without support they become children at risk of school dropout. When they drop out of school, they and society are impacted, including their $10,000 per year diminished earning potential."

While the negative impact is difficult for these children, there can be positive aspects for them. They report stronger family relationships, an increased sense of self-confidence, and feeling valued in their family. For many, school is a respite from their home duties.

In contrast to the UK with its 350 support programs, in the US AACY is the only national resource for caregiving youth. Its local Caregiving Youth Project has demonstrated that with support, lives transform and more than 95 percent of its participants graduate high school with 70 percent going on to post-secondary education. AACY's affiliate network along with its Caregiving Youth Institute that partners with several universities, is furthering its work across the nation. Siskowski, the organization's founder, was recently featured as a CNN Hero for her work.

For more information visit www.aacy.org. If you or an organization in your community would like to support these hidden family heroes, email connie@aacy.org.

Blended Families

Forty-eight percent of all first marriages end in divorce. Remarriage has become commonplace, with the majority of people remarrying within five years of their divorce. Sixty-eight percent or remarriages involve children from previous marriages, so today over 65 percent of Americans are a stepparent, stepchild, stepsibling, or step-grandparent. By 2010 blended families were the most common family type in the US.

Seventy percent of remarriages involving children end in another divorce within 5 years, leaving room for future marriages later in the lives of the children. Fully 43 percent of marriages today involve a second or third remarriage. All of these statistics are likely underestimated, as government reports of population do not specifically track stepfamilies.

In the MetLife *New American Family* report, 17 percent of respondents are part of a blended family, with 75 percent being second marriages and 25 percent domestic partnerships. Though they are older, when their families became blended most had some children who were still financially dependent on them, which in turn created financial responsibility for the new spouse. This is just one of the many issues that occurs as a result of blended relationships.

Couples in first marriages report being more prepared for retirement. Grandparents in first marriages in our survey reported the same. Grandparents in blended families express concern over finances, particularly being fair to one set of children over another; they also have concerns over the way children were raised before their involvement and the residual issues these adult children bring to the relationship. The most successful relationships in our study keep finances separate for discretionary spending and retirement planning.

The MetLife study reports that in second marriages including children, couples are more likely to be concerned with working as long as planned, finding work in retirement, and depleting their savings. Forty-five percent have contributed to the support of a spouse or partner's children. In other words, retirement planning and healthcare are already complex issues for grandparents, and the added layer of a blended family makes it more complicated.

As cited above in the case of grandparent alienation, the grandparents in our study worry about the loss of the relationship with their grandchildren after a divorce. In the case of remarriage of their child, they list acceptance of new step-grandchildren and integration of them into family traditions as their number one and number two concerns. In interviews one grandmother summed up the concerns of many, "You are given a child you didn't meet at birth, from parents you are just getting to know. There isn't a love connection at first! But over time you trust each other and it just works out."

Said another, "Grandchildren are the wealth of old age. Who cares where they came from? I feel lucky to have them all!"

Blended grandparents are very conscious of fairness of spending across all of their grandchildren. They report setting budgets for holiday and birthday spending so grandchildren are treated equally. Spending on grandchildren gets more complicated as children get older and the expenses are larger. Grandparents worry about providing cars and insurance, educational expenses and travel expenses to older grandchildren and their ability to do for all what they might do for one. Just like grandparents in regular families, they frequently spend on their grandchildren's needs, putting their own retirement savings in jeopardy.

CHAPTER SIX

The Rise of the Multi-Generational Household

Multi-generational living is making a comeback after a 35-year low in the 1980s. In 1940 about 25 percent of Americans lived in a household with two generations of adults present. The post-war Baby Boom and the development of the suburbs to house the children of the boom contributed greatly to this style of living falling from favor. Commentators of the day also contributed, focusing on stories of grandparent interference in running the household and raising the children. Around the same period, older people, bolstered by Social Security, were able to live with more financial stability at an older age. By 1980, multigenerational living hit an all time low of 12 percent.

The current upswing is the result of a number of factors. A Pew Research Center analysis of census data reveals, "As of 2008, a record 49 million Americans, or 16.1 percent of the total US population lived in a multigenerational household."

A 2011 study by Generations United found that approximately

one in six Americans resides in a multigenerational household –
a 10 percent jump since the start of the recession.

Figure 18

Share of US population living in multi-generational family households, 1940–2008

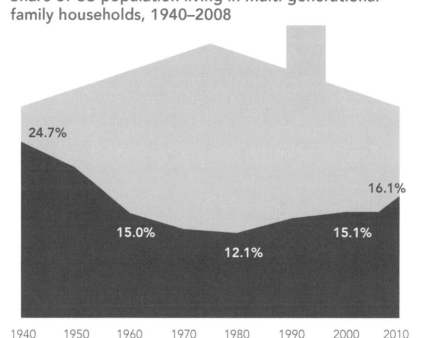

Source: Pew Research Center analysis of the US Decennial Census data, 1940–2000,
and 2006, 2007, 2008 American Community Surveys, based on IPUMS samples

MetLife's *New American Family* study reports, "We have seen
an increase in multi-generational households, which tends to
increase in difficult economic times and fall when the economy
improves. The most recent census confirms that in the past 10
years a record number of parents with small children moved into
their parents' homes, creating a three-generation household.

What differs from the three-generation households of the past is that in most cases the grandparent is the head of household."

Clearly the recession, which began late in 2007, is a major factor in the growth of this lifestyle. Young adults who struggled to launch their careers during this period returned or stayed in the family home in record numbers. People are also marrying later than in previous decades and may choose to remain in their family homes longer. The wave of Hispanic and Asian immigration that began years ago is another contributing factor. Culturally these immigrant populations are more likely to choose a multi-generational living situation than their American-born counterparts. The Black population of American-born people is 10 percent more likely than their White counterparts to be in a multi-generational household.

Figure 19

Share of population in multi-generational family household, by race/ethnicity, 2008

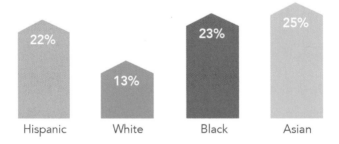

Source: Pew Research Center analysis of 2008 American Community Survey (IPUMS). Hispanics are of any race. White, Black and Asian include only non-Hispanics.

"Kin availability" is a term demographers have coined to describe the phenomenon of older parents having about 50 percent more grown children to share a household with – an artifact of the aging of the Baby Boom generation. Certainly for elderly adults, changes in Medicare and the fear of running out of funds make multi-generational living and the availability of caregivers very attractive.

In two-adult-generation households the older adult is more likely to be the head of the household, at 75 percent. After age 65, this drops to 58 percent, while 42 percent of adult children head the household. Women, especially at the older end of the mature population, are more likely than men to be living this way.

Figure 20

Percent share of population in multi-generational family household, by age and gender, 2008

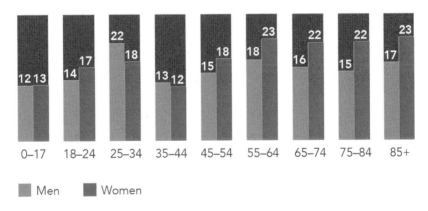

Men   Women

Source: Pew Research Center analysis of 2008 American Community Survey (IPUMS)

Interestingly, young men aged 25 to 34 are just as likely to be living in a multi-generational home as older women.

The MetLife *Grandparents Investing in Grandchildren* study shows that a quarter of the grandparents who report living in a multi-generational household have only their adult children living with them. Only 10 percent report living in their adult child's household.

The "Others" say that none of the traditional multi-generational living styles describe their situation, representing a full 34 percent of the multi-generational households.

Figure 21

Grandparents in multi-generational households

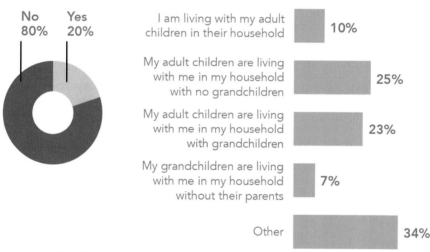

Source: MetLife Mature Market Institute

Multi-generational households spend. In research by Mintel, 60 percent spend more on groceries for children, and 51 percent are spending more on clothing and accessories. These three-generation families would like to be more represented in advertising messages. Thirty-five percent agree that seeing families that look like their own would encourage them to buy products, compared with 29 percent of all parents surveyed.

Grandparents play a critical role in the lives of their grandchildren, but it is easy to underestimate the positive effect they have on their grandchildren because they are there, and we don't think too much about it. The Harvard study mentioned earlier creates a clear link between contentment in old age and having children in their lives. Now a study published in the *Journal of Research on Adolescence,* offers scientific evidence for the contribution of grandparents in children's lives. The study looked at data from more than 400 families with fifth-grade children to determine if the involvement of grandparents has any effect, positive or negative, on a child's development and behavior. They found a correlation between the involvement of grandparents and the development of "kind, helpful and/or empathetic behavior toward others." In other words, grandparents helped shape children into nicer people to be around!

These facts emerged from this study:

- The encouragement of grandparents has a powerful, positive effect on a child's self esteem.

- Interaction with a caring adult outside of the immediate family system helps a child build social skills.

- Children who are close to their grandparents are less likely to experience depression.

- Children view their grandparents as mentors and teachers.

- Children at the adolescent phase of life believe grandparents are more understanding than their parents.

- Children see their grandparents as an important source of advice and support.

- Children say that grandparents matter outside of their relationship with their parents as important people in their lives.

This evidence is enough to support purposeful multi-generational living, as opposed to only need-based. The benefits are clear for both the old and the young, with parents receiving a safety net financially and emotionally.

Caring for Grandchildren

Grandparents have an average of four grandchildren. Fifty-six percent have one or more grandchildren aged 6 to 11, while 53 percent have grandchildren aged five or younger. Twenty-eight percent have grandchildren over age 21. That is a lot of young children!

Historically grandparents have been an important link in the caregiving chain for young families. Parents would prefer to have a family member provide necessary care when given a choice. According to the Census Bureau, grandparents provide care for 23 percent of the nation's preschoolers, which is roughly the same number of children in organized pre-school. Baby Boom generation grandparents have made this more difficult for their children. With this generation of women working longer, there are fewer grandmothers in the home to provide care.

Thirteen percent of grandparents in MetLife's *Grandparents Investing in Grandchildren* survey say they provide care on a regular basis. Grandparents are often responsible for before-and after-school care, and are the default caregivers when a child is sick and parents must work. More than 30 percent of those who provide regular care report providing care five days per week.

Figure 22

Type of care provided for grandchildren (among those who provide care on a regular basis)

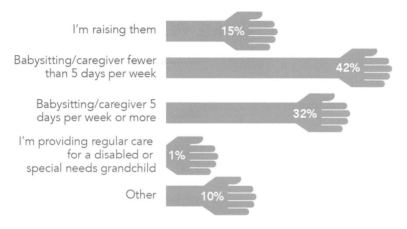

I'm raising them — 15%

Babysitting/caregiver fewer than 5 days per week — 42%

Babysitting/caregiver 5 days per week or more — 32%

I'm providing regular care for a disabled or special needs grandchild — 1%

Other — 10%

Source: MetLife Mature Market Institute

Thirteen percent of grandparents provide care for their grandchildren on a regular basis. More than one-third of those provide care five days per week for their grandchildren.

Younger grandparents – those under age 65 – are most likely to provide care. Fifteen percent of grandmothers provide care regularly, compared with 9 percent of grandfathers.

A new study by Pew Research Center compared the child care and babysitting habits of grandparents in the US, Italy, and Germany. German grandparents are more than twice as likely as American grandparents to have provided regular care. Italian grandparents are almost twice as likely. American grandparents lead in occasional babysitting.

This reflects the differences in a European approach to life, which values leisure and family time highly. Americans are more likely to be working later in life and are less likely to be available to provide care regularly.

Figure 23

US grandparents less likely to provide daily child care
Percent saying they provide child care in the past year

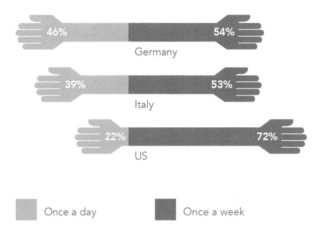

Germany	46%	54%
Italy	39%	53%
US	22%	72%

■ Once a day   ■ Once a week

Note: Based on respondents with at least one grandchild. "Don't know/Refused" responses not shown.

Source: Pew Research Center survey, Oct. 27–Dec. 18, 2014

There are many reasons that grandparents step in to provide care for grandchildren – most importantly because they enjoy it. After the 58 percent who do it for joy is the long list of need-based reasons for providing care. Saving money and allowing parents to work became critically important during the recession. Some grandparents reportedly cut their own work schedules to help provide care for grandchildren. This is another example of grandparents putting their grandchildren's needs ahead of their own need to amass retirement income.

Figure 24

Reasons for providing care (among those who provide care on a regular basis)

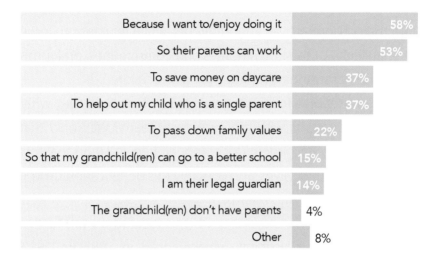

Because I want to/enjoy doing it	58%
So their parents can work	53%
To save money on daycare	37%
To help out my child who is a single parent	37%
To pass down family values	22%
So that my grandchild(ren) can go to a better school	15%
I am their legal guardian	14%
The grandchild(ren) don't have parents	4%
Other	8%

Source: MetLife Mature Market Institute

The majority of grandparents **provide care for the joy of it,** but cite plenty of needs-based reasons as well.

Living Intergenerationally

In 2012, *The New York Times* ran a feature, "The Ultimate Amenity: Grandparents." The story detailed how young New York families, who desire to raise children in the city, are purchasing apartments for their parents and moving them to the city to provide childcare. This was preferred to having parents living with them in their small New York apartments.

The idea of parents providing down payments or buying their offspring New York apartments is fairly common, but this twist is something new. It took a bit of education to get condo directors on board with this new trend – children co-signing for their parents. Leslie Lazarus, a relocation specialist, dubbed it, "in with granny, out with the nanny," while acknowledging that young adult parents want their own parents more integrated into their children's lives. Grandparents, while reluctant to leave the familiarity of their own homes and communities, prefer this to the idea of strangers raising their grandchildren.

While this works for upscale families in New York City, what about grandparents with more modest means? We know that there are reciprocal benefits for grandchildren and grandparents to be in each other's lives, and certainly this benefit shouldn't be reserved for those with means.

Fairhill Partners in Cleveland, Ohio, is located on the former Marine Psychiatric Hospital, which closed in 1983. In 1987, Fairhill Partners took over the property to create a collaborative campus for not-for-profit organizations all focused on the same ideal. The campus is now a Cleveland Historic Landmark, with the mission of connecting people to opportunities for lifelong learning, intergenerational relationships, and successful aging. Over 25 nonprofit, for-profit, and faith-based organizations share space and resources.

In addition to Kinship Care programs for grandparents who are raising their grandchildren, Fairhill has created a nine-unit apartment building designated for kinship families and older adult volunteers. Kinship House is part of Kinship Village, a planned community that promotes successful aging for all and offers a supportive environment for kinship caregivers. In addition to the apartments, Kinship Village includes several townhouses, the former doctors' and officers' quarters when the campus was a Marine hospital. Kinship House apartments are LEED Gold Level Certified.

New Avenue Homes, located in Northern California, has a unique process for helping homeowners add value to their homes through the addition of accessory dwellings. Sometimes called casitas or granny garages, these units are located on the same lot with the family home, providing privacy and independence for grandparents. The cottages that range from 250 to 750 square feet add value to the property and can be used as an office, studio, or guest house as well. They fall into the trendy sweet spot of the "Tiny House" movement.

Several projects have involved the remodeling of the main house for the adult children, followed by the development of

Figure 25

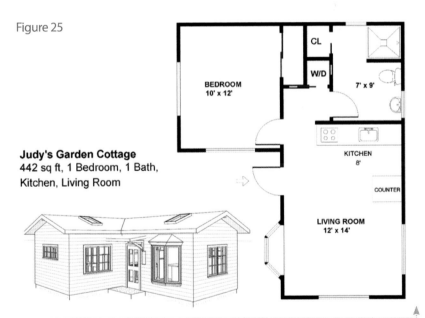

Judy's Garden Cottage
442 sq ft, 1 Bedroom, 1 Bath,
Kitchen, Living Room

This 442 square foot home was built in the backyard of Judy's home in Northern California. Judy remodeled the main house for her daughter and her family, then **built the cottage for herself as a place to live in her retirement.** Until she retires, the cottage is rented to generate a return on their remodeling investment.

a cottage for the grandparents. In a tight housing market with high rents and impossible mortgages, this multigenerational lifestyle is a perfect solution for leveraging an available asset, keeping young families in good established neighborhoods that would otherwise be beyond their means, and supporting the family unit.

Larson Shores architects have developed the brand *Inspired Independence* after finding there were no great solutions for multi-generational living. Their line of "Inspired Homes" are pre-designed new homes that allow multiple generations to live together on the same property, with separation when you want and need it. Architect Carrie Shores is currently chronicling a build in El Cerrito, California on their blog. "Honey" and "Bud" currently live in Ohio, and will be moving to California to live with Deb and Oren and their kids.

The floorplan shows the the shared spaces for living, plus the separate unit with a shared atrium for the grandparents.

Figure 26

Check out the blog for videos and progress of this new project.

● ● ● ● ● ●

CASE STUDY: **NEXTGEN HOMES BY LENNAR**

 Jeff Roos, Regional Vice President of Lennar, ranked the #1 home builder in the nation by *Builder* magazine, calls it a happy accident. He was visiting with an architect in Phoenix when he saw a unique design for a home within a home. It was 2011, in the midst of the foreclosure boom. Roos was looking for an idea that would differentiate the builder in these tough times. He brought the idea back to Lennar, where they did a extensive research on the older consumer and the potential for multi-generational living.

NextGen was born. Unlike a casita or a remodeled garage apartment, NextGen offers a home within a home – all under the same roof. The design creates privacy for the family and the grandparents, but togetherness when they want it. The idea has garnered thousands of dollars of media coverage, with features in *The New York Times, Wall Street Journal,* and *US News & World Report.*

"The beauty of the NextGen home is that it really didn't require a lot of extra investment on the part of Lennar to make it work. Once we had the designs, building it and refining it became a passion," said Roos. "The NextGen suite features a private entrance, master suite, eat-in kitchenette, laundry and living room. Many have their own patio for cooking out and their own garages."

EVOLUTION
Approximately 2,958 Square Feet
Single Level • 4 Bedrooms• 3 Bathrooms

This beautiful one story NEXT GEN® home includes; A main home and a private suite that are seamlessly connected with a dual access door; similar to adjoining hotel rooms, which allows for as much interaction between the main home and the private suite as you desire.

Since 2011, Lennar has built 2,700 NextGen homes in 20 markets across 10 states. There are currently more than 40 floor plans in 100 communities. Imitators have emerged, but Lennar has a clear first mover advantage and a lot of learning under its belt. In several markets, for example, they are learning and adapting to the preferences of different cultures, like Indian and Chinese elders.

Roos reports that Lennar is evolving the concept and expanding throughout the US. They are looking at the reviews from current homeowners and adding features like enhanced storage and trending ideas. They have also developed tools to help prospective buyers understand the actual savings of putting two homes under a single roof.

"It's rewarding," continued Roos. "These homes change the dynamic of families. We have had homeowners in tears as they tell us they no longer have to drive across town to provide care for their parents, or have multiple generations of people living on top of each other. Relationships are better. Grandparents are helping kids with homework."

"We are also hearing that it has been a great investment for families. And in addition to providing space for grandparents, we are seeing families use this for disabled adult children, returning veterans who require assistance and those suffering from PTSD. NextGen is a game-changing concept."

Intergenerational Life

The United States is experiencing a demographic transformation. We are becoming a nation of very young and very old people. By 2030 there will be 72 million people over age 65, and 80 million children aged 0 to 17. By 2040 older adults and children will comprise 40 percent of the US population. Currently aging services organizations are seeing cuts in funding as foundations seek opportunities to help young children. Without investment in intergenerational programs we are on a collision course of old versus young.

Intergenerational programs are designed to bring together children and older adults in a planned, mutually beneficial, and ongoing way. Unlike "multi-generational" the term "intergenerational" does not include people who are related. Probably the best known intergenerational program, Foster Grandparents, turns 50-years old this year. The idea is for people of all ages to share their talent and resources, and also support each other for their own benefit and that of the greater community. In many ways intergenerational programs are a response to a society that has become highly segregated by age.

We work, live and learn in age-segmented ways. We do not frequently bring together people of all ages, socioeconomic backgrounds, races, and ethnicities. As a result, people along the age continuum have become socially isolated. Intergenerational programs mix ages, experience, and wisdom, and result in fresh ideas and points of view.

Generations United, a proponent of intergenerational programming, believes: "Bridging communities improves lives and communities. We can solve real problems and build connections among generations and their communities. The result is that life gets better for all of us."

In fact, Generations United and MetLife Foundation honor the best intergenerational communities with an annual awards program. Intergenerational communities are not just places where multiple generations live. People of all ages are considered integral and valued community members. Structures, facilities, and services in the community reflect respect for the youngest and oldest members. One of the hallmarks is the high quality partnership between the public and private sectors to create a community that benefits people of every age and encourages interaction.

Older people may work as mentors, school tutors, and child care providers. They report lower levels of disability, higher levels of happiness, and reduced depression. Most of all they are able to apply their skills and wisdom to feel like productive and contributing members of their community. Older adults often provide their talent in a learning environment. There is an intergenerational charter school movement that appreciates the growing number of talented older adults in the population and the huge need young people have for social, emotional, and academic support.

Children help with household chores, visit with older adults, and serve as reverse mentors for teaching technology. Children benefit from feeling productive, gain confidence in their skills, develop a strong sense of community, and learn to value older adults. Psychologist Susan Pinker writes, "Children thrive on face-to-face contact with caring adults. Indeed there is no substitute for such connection when it comes to everything from language through development."

Social innovator and CEO of encore.org, Marc Freedman said it best and shared a model for intergenerational living ". . . age-segregated housing for retirees runs against the grain of everything we know about healthy development in the post-midlife period, a time when connections with younger generations are linked to higher rates of happiness for older people. What we need instead: housing strategies that help to forge and solidify bonds among the generations."

"One compelling example is Bridge Meadows. This housing development in Portland, Oregon, brings together families raising foster children with older people of modest means, who receive reduced rents in return for volunteer work with the adoptive families living in the community: everything from baby sitting and playing catch with children to working on arts-and-crafts projects and making meals. It's an arrangement that makes both economic and common sense, filling the fundamental human need for community and connection."

CHAPTER SEVEN

The Grandparent Lifestyle: Technology & Connection

Technology and the speed of change may be the key difference between today's grandparents and grandchildren, and those of past generations. The pervasive nature of screen life has changed every aspect of life from work to leisure time. While Boomer-age adults have adapted to the advent and rise of technology in their lives from the beginning, their grandchildren are digital natives, never having known life any other way. Grandchildren will never know the exercise in patience of waiting for the next installment of a favorite television program, or the weekly phone call from home during their college years. They only know and understand immediacy and on-demand.

Brain scientists have shown that use of technology literally rewires the brain. For example, reliance on GPS and mapping apps is changing those parts of our brains that help us navigate and problem solve. Grandchildren are exposed to screens as infants. Technology is omnipresent in their lives.

Grandparents worry about the effect of technology on children. In our study 88 percent of grandparents revealed that they believe technology has assumed too large a role in daily lives. One grandfather interviewed said, "I joke with my 13-year-old granddaughter about how straight the part in her hair is . . . because it's all I see when she's glued to her iPhone – which we bought for her. When she's with us, she isn't really present. I worry about the outcome. Honestly, I've talked to my daughter about it, but she is almost as bad!"

A single grandmother believes she has found a solution, "I have two grandsons who are seven and nine. They hang out with me on a couple of weekends a month. They live in town and I have a place at the beach, so they still think I'm fun! I know this time is precious. The oldest already has lots of commitments with his soccer and baseball. It may be selfish, but when they are here I want them "here." They bring their video games when they come, but I control their time with them. I don't think kids spend enough time outside. I read an article about kids having a nature deficit and I think it's true. I plan one day of outdoor stuff every time they come. We've gone fishing, we have hiked the state park, we've spent an entire day on the beach with a picnic, and we ride bikes all around the little town here. The games are at home in a basket on the breakfast bar. When they are outside and relaxed, they are still little boys. We talk about everything. They get their games back for an hour while I make dinner, then we do something together like a movie or a board game. And I don't allow the games in the car. I don't want them to think being in a car with distractions is ok. My son thinks I'm over the top, but it just feels right to me and the boys don't complain – at least to me!"

Another grandmother told us she purchased an iPhone because of her 12-year-old granddaughter. "I had my cell phone for seven years. My kids told me it was 'old school' but I didn't need a camera or texting. My grandbaby has started worrying about how she looks. I was worried about an eating disorder or her comparing herself to some of these young actresses and models. She's sort of shy and quiet. Her mom decided to get her a phone for her birthday. She was showing me all of these apps she had found. One of them is a fitness thing that tracks all of your fitness activities. So I decided to get a phone, too. We made a plan. I got the same fitness app – which she showed me how to do. Now we walk or run together and share our activities. It's been fun. She showed me how to text and use maps. She sends me 'selfies' when she's working out. She seems more open and confident. And of course she looks beautiful and healthy. It's been really good for both of us!"

Along with the good comes the bad, as this grandmother shared, "My grandson is three and his mom and dad live for their technology. They have everything you can think of, but my son works in technology, so it makes sense. They make videos of him and take lots of photos of him. Everything is on their Instagram account. Sometimes I see more of him on Facebook than I do in person. I worry about how much they share about him. He's too little to make a choice about sharing. Everyone says this stuff is out there forever. Do we want a picture of him peeing in his wading pool to follow him to college?"

And this, "I think my four year old granddaughter is turning into a technology brat. Her mom puts her iPad in front of her whenever she wants to settle her down, or her phone when she's desperate. She plays little games and watches videos, but whenever she's bored or not getting attention she wants, she screams for her 'shows.' Her mom calls her a diva and thinks it's cute. To me this is just their generation's version of plopping kids in front of a TV when you can't manage them. I think it will lead to big problems."

While grandparents worry about the negative effects of technology, they also embrace it as a way to stay in touch with their grandchildren, even when they live in close proximity. The recent Pew Research Center report, *Keeping in Touch Across Generations,* shows that 20 percent of US grandparents communicate with their grandchildren once a day, and 19 percent communicate less than once a month or never. (This study does not include grandparents living with a grandchild.) Forty-one percent communicate once a week with a grandchild, and another 19 percent say once a month. (See Figure 27) This study compares grandparenting connections for Italian, US, and German grandparents. Italian grandparents are twice as likely to connect with their grandchildren on a daily basis, reflecting the close family ties in their culture. US grandparents are also most likely to not communicate with grandchildren at all.

When grandparents are asked how they communicate with grandchildren, the phone still wins. But email, Facebook, texting and Skype are also important.

Ten percent of grandparents still write letters to their grandchildren. While the grandparents in our study like the immediacy and visual quality of connecting via technology, 43 percent lament the death of the posted letter. Many said that

Figure 27

Italian grandparents in close contact with grandchildren
Percent saying they are in contact with their grandchild/grandchildren at least…

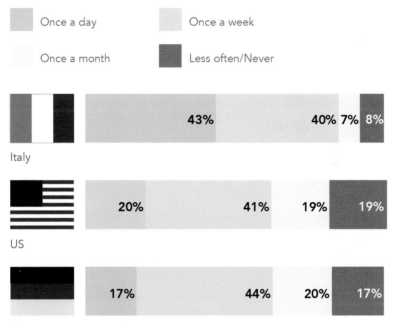

Note: Based on adults with at least one grandchild. Respondents were asked to think only about relatives who do not live with them. Those who volunteered that their grandchild/grandchildren live with them were excluded from the analysis. "Don't know/Refused" not shown.

Source: Pew Research Center survey, Oct. 27–Dec. 18, 2014

While 20% of US grandparents have daily contact with their grandchildren, **more than twice as many Italian grandparents do so**.

their grandchildren love getting real mail. Grandparents send funny pictures (often printed from the internet), cards, and share anecdotes.

Figure 28

How do they communicate?

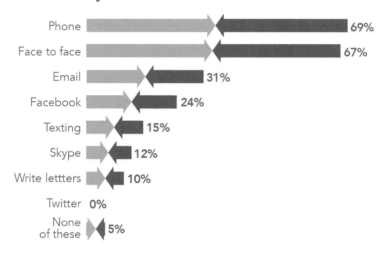

Source: MetLife Mature Market Institute

> Grandparents prefer face time with their grandchildren, but if they can't be with them, the **phone still ranks number one** for communicating.

Fifty-six percent of grandmothers in our study revealed that they started using Facebook because they were interested in seeing what their adult children were posting about their grand-children, or that they were following their grandchild. Twenty-six percent were led to Skype or FaceTime by their adult children, typically living more than 100 miles or more away, to provide regular communication with their grandchildren. Seventy-one percent of grandparents expressed frustration over not receiv-ing actual photographs of their grandchildren anymore. "My daughter tells me to download them off of Facebook! That's easy for her to say. I don't have time to figure that out." Another says she was lunching with friends recently and everyone was passing around phones to look at photos of their grandchildren – the modern equivalent of Grandma's Brag Book.

Figure 29

**How do grandparents keep in touch with their grandchildren?
Mainly over the telephone.**
Percent saying they typically communicate with their grandchild/ grandchildren by…

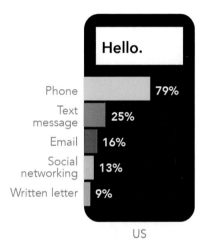

Phone	79%
Text message	25%
Email	16%
Social networking	13%
Written letter	9%

US

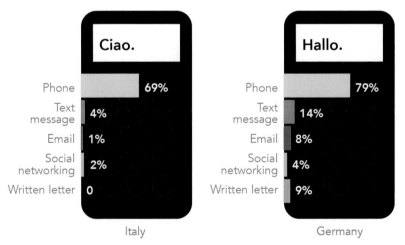

Ciao.

Phone	69%
Text message	4%
Email	1%
Social networking	2%
Written letter	0

Italy

Hallo.

Phone	79%
Text message	14%
Email	8%
Social networking	4%
Written letter	9%

Germany

Note: Based on adults with at least one grandchild with whom they are in contact at least once a month. Email and social networking items were asked only of adults who use those outlets, but percentages here are based on total.

Source: Pew Research Center survey, Oct. 27–Dec. 18, 2014

In the Pew study, US grandparents are much more likely to text, use email and social networks than their European counterparts.

This may be reflective of the size of the US, versus Italy or Germany, and number of grandparents who are not local to their grandchildren.

Figure 30

Percentage of grandparents who have one or more grandchildren by distance

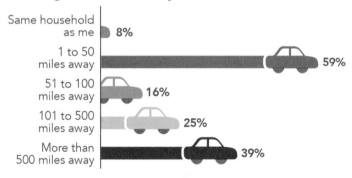

Source: AARP

Brands That Help Grandparents Connect

There is a lot of room for new companies to help grandparents better connect with their grandchildren. In our study, Apple stood out as the clear winner, with 66 percent of grandparents saying that FaceTime was an important innovation for connection. Facebook came in at 31 percent, with many more grandmothers than grandfathers citing it. Skype came in at 22 percent, with more grandfathers than grandmothers choosing it. An honorable mention goes to Hallmark for its recordable books that allow grandparents to read a bedtime story, record it and give it to their grandchildren to listen to when they aren't there.

When asked for information sources that help them navigate the grandparent lifestage, grandmothers listed Babycenter.com, grandparents.com and *GRAND Magazine*. Less than 5 percent listed *AARP Magazine*, which was surprising. Daughters and daughter-in-laws ranked just under online sites in terms of importance. Peers who are grandparents were by far the number one source of information for today's grandparents.

Health & Wellness

The majority of Boomer-aged grandparents report that they are in good to very good health, in spite of the fact that more than 50 percent are managing two or more chronic conditions. Sixty-four percent of grandparents in our study said the birth of their first grandchild was a time to reflect on their health. In interviews, grandparents said they changed their health habits to be in their grandchild's life longer and to set a good example for their grandchild. This includes changes in eating habits, getting more exercise, and trying to deal more effectively with stress.

In spite of what Boomers believe about their health, they are not aging more healthily than previous generations. A Pew study, *The Diagnosis Difference*, shows that Boomers have the same rates of high blood pressure, heart conditions, and lung conditions as previous generations. They are on track for higher levels of diabetes. A study by the Journal of the American Medical Association, *The Status of Baby Boomers Health in the United States: The Healthiest Generation,* shows that this generation is less likely to be smoking, are more likely to be obese, have hypertension, diabetes, and high cholesterol. In fact, people aged 70 plus report more time spent on exercise and nutrition than younger generations. As Boomers work longer, they are on track for higher rates of hypertension and heart conditions.

Businesses are banking on Boomer health issues. AARP reports that healthcare spending currently tops $1.6 trillion. Investment in technology for improving health outcomes in the Boomer demographic continues to soar.

Brands are leveraging the size of the Boomer market and

Boomer's desire to improve their health in the most painless way possible. Both Kellogg's and General Mills shifted their breakfast brands to a heart-health platform. Kellogg's has created grandparent-centric messaging around its legacy brands – All-Bran, Rice Krispies, and Corn Flakes.

Healthcare giant, UnitedHealthcare has run an ongoing campaign against childhood obesity that targets grandparents.

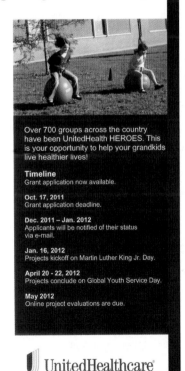

UnitedHealth HEROES^{SM}

Help your grandkids fight against obesity!

Here's your chance to help tackle one of our most pressing health issues – childhood obesity.

UnitedHealthcare is collaborating with YSA (Youth Service America) for the fourth year to offer UnitedHealth HEROES, a program that provides grants to support innovative projects that address childhood obesity.

The applicant must be:

- a teacher or service-learning* coordinator at a public, faith-based, or charter school; or
- student(s) in the health professions; or
- staff at a community-based non-profit organization.

How to apply

Visit www.YSA.org/HEROES to apply now!

Applications must be submitted online by midnight EST on Oct. 17, 2011.

For questions regarding this grant program, e-mail healthheroes@ysa.org.

*Service-learning is a teaching and learning strategy that integrates academic study with meaningful service to the community.

Over 700 groups across the country have been UnitedHealth HEROES. This is your opportunity to help your grandkids live healthier lives!

Timeline
Grant application now available.

Oct. 17, 2011
Grant application deadline.

Dec. 2011 – Jan. 2012
Applicants will be notified of their status via e-mail.

Jan. 16, 2012
Projects kickoff on Martin Luther King Jr. Day.

April 20 - 22, 2012
Projects conclude on Global Youth Service Day.

May 2012
Online project evaluations are due.

Insurance coverage provided by or through UnitedHealthcare Insurance Company or its affiliates. Administrative services provided by UnitedHealthcare Insurance Company, United HealthCare Services, Inc. or their affiliates.

Consumer © 2011 United HealthCare Services, Inc.

UnitedHealthcare®

The grant program appeals to Boomers concern over their grandchildren's health and their desire to do greater good in their communities.

Other than a large health event, like a heart attack, the birth of a grandchild remains the biggest catalyst for changes in health habits. One grandfather put it like this, "I love golf and baseball. My son-in-law has no time with his job and his commute to do these things on a regular basis with my twin grandsons who are eight. When I first started working with them I discovered I was really out of shape! I had a hard time keeping up with two little guys. I put myself into training and dropped 27 pounds. We are eating much better – we've got to be good examples! I'm eating vegetables. After 7 months I am off of Lipitor and my joints don't ache in the morning because I'm dragging around extra weight. Now we've got a granddaughter on the way! I'm motivated!"

Sex, Drugs and Rock & Roll

While alcohol is part of the culture of generations past, Boomers made it part of popular culture. The beer, wine and spirits industries soared as Boomers came of age and centered their social life around the consumption of alcohol. Unfortunately with age come changes to the way the body metabolizes alcohol. DUI incidents in the group aged 50 to 65 have nearly doubled in the last decade. Many Boomers who drank heavily in their young adult years backed off in their 30s and 40s as they raised their children. Now free of parental responsibilities the majority of Boomers have resumed their culture of social drinking. Most Boomers do not believe regular drinking is a problem.

Substance abuse issues are also on the rise. Rehabilitation

Figure 31A

Counterculture generation brings drug habits into middle age

Accidental drug overdose rates for people 45–64 have risen sharply as Baby Boomers, a generation with a predilection for drugs, have gotten older in an era of prescription pill abuse.

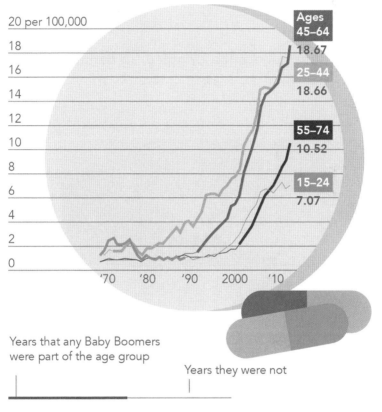

Years that any Baby Boomers were part of the age group

Years they were not

Source: *Wall Street Journal*

programs are retooling for a boom in Boomers. By 2020 it is estimated that 5.7 million people over age 50 will require treatment. Experts believe that the generation is predisposed to substance abuse. The Substance Abuse and Mental Health

Services Administration's annual survey of drug use finds marijuana and painkillers to be the Boomer drugs of choice. Medical marijuana and legalization of recreational marijuana have made it much easier for Boomers to continue their habit. The issue has become so pervasive that senior living communities and skilled nursing facilities find themselves in the position of creating policies for the use of marijuana.

Figure 31B

Counterculture generation brings drug habits into middle age

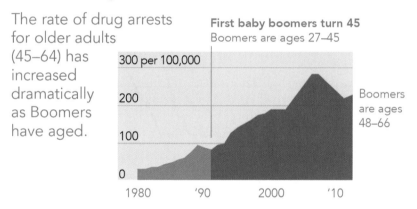

The rate of drug arrests for older adults (45–64) has increased dramatically as Boomers have aged.

First baby boomers turn 45
Boomers are ages 27–45

300 per 100,000
200
100
0

Boomers are ages 48–66

1980   '90   2000   '10

Source: *Wall Street Journal*

The aches and pains of aging have exacerbated the issue. Injuries and recovery on pain medication have lead to addiction for some Boomers. Accidental overdoses in the Boomer age range are now higher than the 25-to-44-year-old age range. Arrests rates have continued to rise as well. Boomers who mix alcohol and painkillers have more risk of a fatal event. Rehabilitation facilities are struggling to help older addicts who truly believe that drug use in general is not problematic.

The implications for the healthcare system are broad.

According to the federal Agency for Healthcare Research and Quality, 45-to-64-year-olds had the highest rate of hospital stays for opioid abuse in 2012. Emergency room visits for older adults who are mixing alcohol, painkillers and cocaine contain to rise. Data on female addicts in the Boomer cohort is an under-reported problem as older women tend to cover their habits and drink alone.

While grandparents report sharing values as an important role in their grandchildren's lives, they are unclear about how to handle the topic of alcohol and drugs with them. In our survey, the majority feel that teaching grandchildren moderation is important. A minority believes that their experience with alcohol and drugs is not relevant to their grandchild relationships. More than 80 percent report being conflicted about this topic when it comes to their grandchildren.

Sexual activity in later life is also different for this generation of older adults. Viagra has contributed to improved sex lives for older adults. It is also blamed for a rise in sexually transmitted diseases in people over age 50. The incidence of syphilis and chlamydia in adults aged 45-to-64 tripled from 2000 to 2010 according to the Center for Disease Control. In states like Florida and Arizona where the older population is higher than average, the rates are much higher. A study in *Journal of Sexual Medicine* looked at the sexual habits of older adults and discovered that 91 percent of men over age 50 report not using condoms during sex; almost 60 percent of women do not. Sexual activity is yet another issue that senior living and skilled nursing facilities are grappling with as they welcome a different type of senior through their doors.

Unlike alcohol and drugs, grandparents believe that their grandchildren should be taught about sex in an age appropriate way throughout their lives so that they approach their teens and twenties responsibly. Eighty-two percent of grandparents support sexual health education for teenagers. The majority of grandparents do not believe their sexual history or health is relevant to their relationship with their grandchild. Only three in ten would be willing to share information to help their grandchild navigate his or her own sexual landscape.

To complete the triumvirate, rock and roll continues to flourish thanks to the disposable income of the Baby Boom generation. Reunion tour concerts, merchandising, downloads, and streaming music have all realized the benefit of the Boomer love for great music. Boomer grandparents share their love of music with a new generation through their grandchildren. Young artists continue to mine the song books of older artists to cover great songs and put their own twist on them for a new audience.

Younger artists targeting the tween and teen markets are also reaping the rewards, as Boomer grandparents report purchasing concert tickets, merchandise, and backstage experiences for their grandchildren.

The Un-retirement Plan

Three trillion dollars in buying power is attractive to any CMO. The older adult demographic outpaces younger demographics in wealth accumulation. According to Pew Research Center this gap will continue to grow. Median net worth in households of persons aged 35 and under declined 44 percent from 1984–2011, and rose 37 percent in the age-85-plus segment. In

2011, the wealth of older adult households was 26 times that of younger households.

The recession exacerbated the issue as younger workers experienced higher unemployment rates than older workers. Those who did find employment saw the largest declines in earnings. Even as the economy recovers, younger workers have the biggest gap to fill. Forty-five percent of parents say they feel obligated to help their children regain their financial footing.

Still middle-and lower-income Boomers saw the effect of the recession. They saw job losses, stayed unemployed longer, and spent down their savings. Many say it has had a lasting effect on their ability to retire when they thought they would.

Figure 32

Half of grandparents have provided financial assistance to their adult children

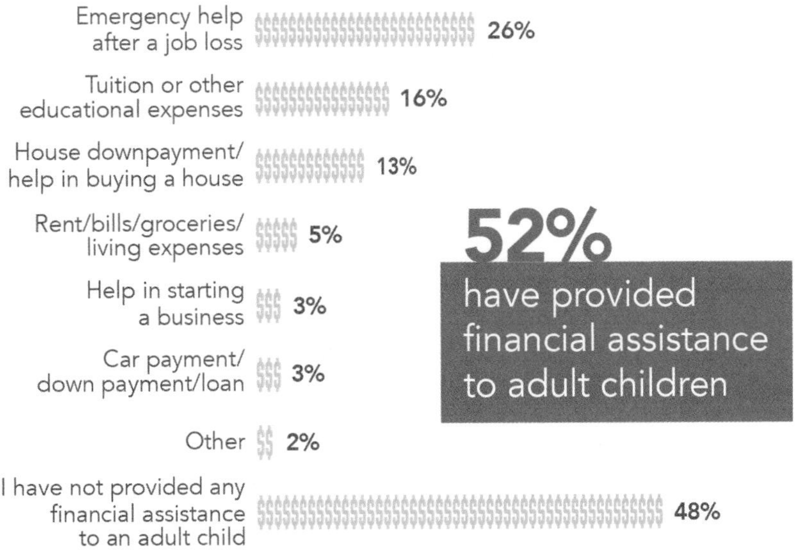

Emergency help after a job loss — 26%

Tuition or other educational expenses — 16%

House downpayment/ help in buying a house — 13%

Rent/bills/groceries/ living expenses — 5%

Help in starting a business — 3%

Car payment/ down payment/loan — 3%

Other — 2%

I have not provided any financial assistance to an adult child — 48%

52% have provided financial assistance to adult children

Source: MetLife Mature Market Institute

Studies by AARP and MetLife find that that grandparents, in spite of their own financial condition, continued to provide assistance to their adult children. Fifty-two percent have provided financial assistance that ranges from help after a job loss to basic living expenses.

Twenty percent of respondents in the MetLife *New American Family* study worried that retirement dollars could be jeopardized by the healthcare needs of other family members.

Thirty-four percent are giving financial support to their grandchildren while acknowledging the negative impact on their own security.

Figure 33

Financial assistance from grandparents

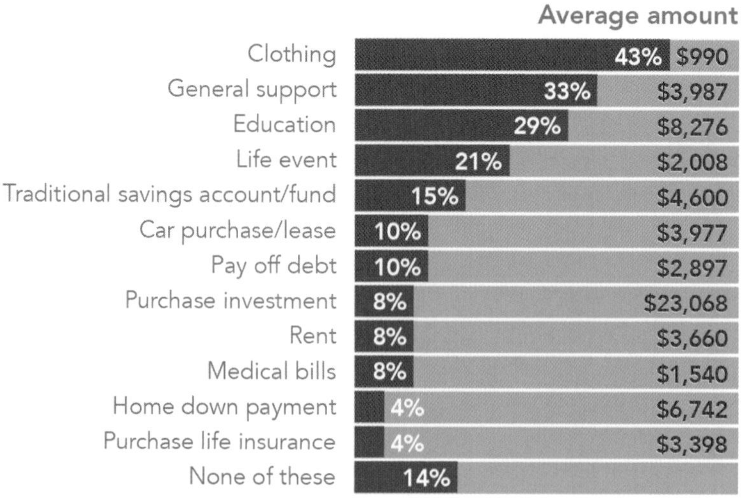

	Percent	Average amount
Clothing	43%	$990
General support	33%	$3,987
Education	29%	$8,276
Life event	21%	$2,008
Traditional savings account/fund	15%	$4,600
Car purchase/lease	10%	$3,977
Pay off debt	10%	$2,897
Purchase investment	8%	$23,068
Rent	8%	$3,660
Medical bills	8%	$1,540
Home down payment	4%	$6,742
Purchase life insurance	4%	$3,398
None of these	14%	

Source: MetLife Mature Market Institute

Grandparents are financing much more than vacations and peak experiences. They are increasingly **financing more expenses of daily living** for their adult children and grandchildren.

As Figure 33 illustrates, spending on grandchildren covers a broad range of expenses. Where grandparents of previous generations generally spent infrequently, and on big-ticket items on gifting occasions, the Boomer generation is spending regularly, covering expenses traditionally paid for by parents.

While funding retirement is the number one concern for 61 percent of Americans, relatively little financial planning is taking place. In a Gallup report, three out of four people say they will work past traditional retirement age. One-third of those will work out of need. Interestingly, the higher the level of education and the higher the level of salary, the more likely Boomers are to say they will continue to work at least five years past the traditional retirement age of 65.

The workforce will continue to age, and not all will work out of financial need. Many Boomer-age employees say they work for the satisfaction and sense of purpose their employment provides. Boomer women, in particular, have reached the peak of their career and earning years and show no desire to slow down now. In 2013, more workers aged 65-plus were working versus the past three years of reporting. For today's grandparents the retirement plan seems to be putting their heads down and working longer, even as they provide the safety net for the rest of their family.

Leading Charitable Gifts

Even with the financial maelstrom of the recession, Baby Boomers lead charitable giving. Older generations have traditionally filled the coffers of non-profit organizations; now Boomers are stepping in to fill the gaps.

Figure 34

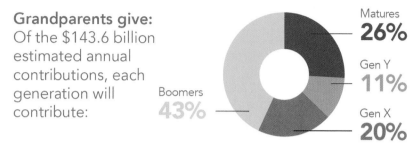

Grandparents give:
Of the $143.6 billion estimated annual contributions, each generation will contribute:

Boomers
43%

Matures
26%

Gen Y
11%

Gen X
20%

Boomers lead giving:

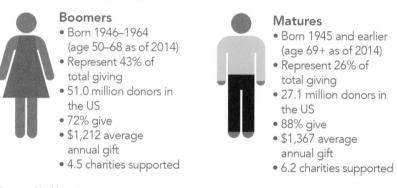

Boomers
- Born 1946–1964 (age 50–68 as of 2014)
- Represent 43% of total giving
- 51.0 million donors in the US
- 72% give
- $1,212 average annual gift
- 4.5 charities supported

Matures
- Born 1945 and earlier (age 69+ as of 2014)
- Represent 26% of total giving
- 27.1 million donors in the US
- 88% give
- $1,367 average annual gift
- 6.2 charities supported

Source: Blackbaud

Boomers give a total of $61.9 billion annually, making up 43 percent of annual giving. With an average give of $1,212 in charitable contributions, they give at nearly twice the rate of younger demographics.

Once a Boomer becomes a grandparent they report that their giving habits change. Local organizations, particularly those that touch their grandchildren's lives, become a higher priority than national campaign contributions. The exception is children's charities and causes, which seem to touch the grandparent's heartstrings once they have grandchildren. Grandparents also report giving heavily to their grandchildren's school and sports fundraising activities.

CHAPTER EIGHT

The Last Word on Grandparent Spending

This book is about the incredible contribution that grandparents are making in the lives of their grandchildren, financially, socially and emotionally. It is also a "how to" for companies that want to speak fluently to the lucrative grandparent lifestage. It is fitting that we end with a look at where grandparent dollars are going and some of the spending trends we have identified in our research.

The annual Bureau of Labor Statistics report on child-related items is a good place to start. It tracks spending for:

- Baby food, infant equipment, and clothing

- Toys, games, and tricycles

- Elementary and Secondary school tuition and supplies

Over a ten-year period, spending on the first two categories saw an increase of more than 71 percent, or $7.6 billion. Figure 35 illustrates that spending in these categories rose sharply when compared with household income. Also important is the fact that spending for these items in households with children

– those aged 25-to-34 and 35-to-44 – saw a decline in spending for these categories, supporting the theory that grandparents are picking up the slack when it comes to necessities for their grandchildren.

Figure 35

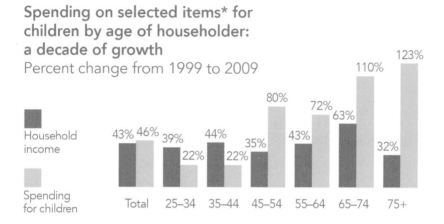

Spending on selected items* for children by age of householder: a decade of growth
Percent change from 1999 to 2009

*Selected items include baby food, infant clothes and equipment, toys and games, plus elementary and secondary school tuition and supplies.

Source: Bureau of Labor Statistics Consumer Expenditure Surveys, MetLife Mature Market Institute

The third category, spending on elementary and secondary schools, has seen tremendous growth. Spending rose from $981 million in 1999 – 2.5 times – to $2.43 billion. This spending increase reflects the Boomers' focus on education and the importance they place on their grandchildren's future.

MetLife reports that grandparent households spend heavily on insurance. With more assets to insure and more income to invest in insurance products, this is a natural category of spending. It is also a category of investment used for those who are less financially savvy and more risk averse. There is also evidence that grandparents are spending on cars and auto insurance for their adult children and grandchildren. The Consumer Expenditure Survey by BLS shows an increase in spending for auto insurance by households 55 and older.

Figure 36

Spending on home and auto insurance per household: Percent change 2000–2009

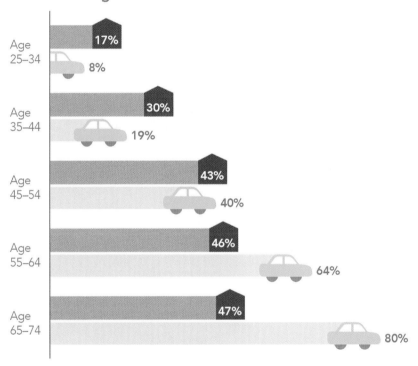

Age 25–34: 17% / 8%

Age 35–44: 30% / 19%

Age 45–54: 43% / 40%

Age 55–64: 46% / 64%

Age 65–74: 47% / 80%

Note: US average: home +45%, auto +38%, CPI: 25%

Source: Bureau of Labor Statistics Consumer Expenditure Surveys, MetLife Mature Market Institute

Large increases in spending for auto insurance among older consumers, coupled with the relatively small increases by adult children and young adults, would indicate that **grandparents are covering insurance for younger generations of drivers.**

Fifty-five plus spending on used cars given as gifts rose from $224 million in 2000 to $863 million in 2009, likely given to adult children or teenage grandchildren.

In an AARP Study, *Insights and Spending Habits of Modern Grandparents,* 96 percent of grandparents say they spend money on their grandchildren. The majority of those do so for the joy of giving to them. The most common reasons for giving

Figure 37

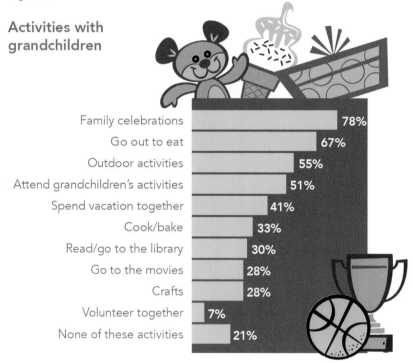

Activities with grandchildren

Activity	Percentage
Family celebrations	78%
Go out to eat	67%
Outdoor activities	55%
Attend grandchildren's activities	51%
Spend vacation together	41%
Cook/bake	33%
Read/go to the library	30%
Go to the movies	28%
Crafts	28%
Volunteer together	7%
None of these activities	21%

Source: AARP

Grandparents **balance spending time and money** with their grandchildren. The activities they cite are low to no cost. The importance of sharing interests and values is illustrated here.

are holidays, and birthdays. They also spend on entertainment/ fun (82 percent), educational expenses (53 percent), everyday expenses (37 percent) and medical/dental expenses (23 percent).

Fifty-five percent of participants said the economy has not affected their spending on their grandchildren. They will cut back in other places because their grandchildren are a higher priority. "We still spend on our grandchild, but it makes a bigger impact on us than it did in the past," said one interviewee. "I was laid off in October, but I try not to have the situation affect my grandchildren," said another.

A look at the ways grandparents spend time with their grandchildren provides a great roadmap to spending.

Figure 37 illustrates the top activities cited by grandparents. What is striking is the balance between activities that cost money, like eating out, movies and vacations, versus modest activities like volunteer work, outdoor activities, and the library.

The travel industry has focused recently on grandparent and multi-generational travel. Road Scholar provides special adventures for grandparents traveling with grandchildren, with a focus on educational and historical benefits. Disney Cruise Line provides cruising opportunities that offer something for every member of the multi-generational family. Go RVing encourages family and multi-generational camping experiences across the US.

Travel is an important spending category because it appeals to the older adult's experiential nature, allows them to teach and mentor their grandchildren, and creates memories with their families.

● ● ● ● ● ● ● ● ● ● ● ● ● ● ● ● ● ● ●

A Tradition of Travel

Rebecca and Milton have four grandchildren from their three children. They now range in age from 9 to 16. When Michael, the oldest, turned 12 Rebecca and Milton decided to start a tradition. They would plan and take a trip with each grandchild during their 12th year, to a destination of their chosing (within reason).

"It has been interesting to see what the kids come up with as ideas. We put a lot of emphasis on planning the trip because we get to talk to them for a couple of years leading up to the actual trip. We share emails. They send away for information. We put a lot of the responsibility in their hands," said Rebecca, who has now experienced three of these excursions. Her husband Milton passed away unexpectedly before the third trip with their granddaughter Alex.

"We went anyway. It was about a month and a half after Milt died. He would have wanted us to go."

So far, the trips have included Brazil with Michael, England and France with Caden, and Alaska and Vancouver with Angela. Everett who is now nine is narrowing down his ideas. He studies Spanish language in school, so Spain or Mexico are still on his list, though Cuba is emerging as a choice.

"We are fortunate," says Rebecca. "We worked hard to provide these experiences for our grandkids. Milton and I believe that they need to be citizens of a bigger world and we can help them learn. It's been interesting to see how these trips have changed them. Our oldest, Michael, is interested in International Business and living in Brazil when he is in college. He was very taken with our Rain Forest excursion, too."

"Caden wants to be a designer, so our trip to France and England was all about fashion and art – much to Milt's chagrin! He loved it, but he wasn't much of a shopper! And the cruise to Alasksa with Angie was very special for us both. We reminisced about Milt and spent a lot of time outdoors. She's a wonderful photographer, so we have a great album. I'm secretly hoping that Everett will pick Cuba! It will be a huge adventure."

"While we started doing this for the kids, it's been great for us. We have had time with each of the kids, not just on the trip but while we were planning. We get to see how they think about the world, the way they plan, what matters to them. And especially since Milton is gone, they've made me brave! No way I'm going to let even one of them down. These are my memories too!"

First-time grandparents are the focus of home décor companies focused on luxurious nurseries and children's spaces. Frequently grandparents purchase the nursery furniture for the grandchildren, and also furnish some items for their own homes. In the past 10 years, every major furniture retailer has introduced a children's line to capture grandparent dollars. Crate &

Barrel introduced The Land of Nod; Pottery Barn has the trendy Pottery Barn Kids and PB Teens; Ethan Allen Kids and Teens; and Restoration Hardware Baby. These purchase decisions are driven by adult children, but purchased by grandparents. Even discount retailer Target has a line of trendy children's décor.

Forty-three percent of grandparents purchase clothing for their grandchildren, spending an average of nearly $1,000 annually. With $400 billion in spending on goods and services, people aged 55 and older are not just spending in stores. A new report from Bronto Software shows they are outspending younger consumers two to one online. Seventeen percent shop online on a weekly basis, while 38 percent spend monthly. Tablet penetration has grown from 35 percent to 41 percent in this segment, and they account for one in four mobile transactions.

Children's clothing retailers are reaping the benefit of grandparent spending. While grandparents appreciate department store shopping, they shop online with higher end children's specialty stores like GAP Baby and Gap Kids and crewcuts by J. Crew, and sale sites like Zulily that focus on kids clothing and toys. Further, these companies target grandparents on social media and targeted websites.

Grandfathers are getting into the spending act. Big box home-improvement stores like Home Depot and Lowes target parents and grandparents and their children with simple building project activities in their stores. Outdoor retailers like Cabela's and Bass Pro Shops also plan demonstrations and activities for families in their stores. These stores play into a grandfather's desire to share skills and hobbies with his grandchildren.

Culture Vultures

Grandparents have assumed the role of the keepers of the family traditions. This extends to managing and paying for family celebrations like birthdays and Christmas.

Figure 38

Grandparents are "Culture Vultures"
Grandparents are the keepers of traditions and take on the role of managing family celebrations.

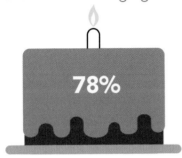

Grandparents selected family celebrations as the most important activity with grandchildren

Find it important to share their heritage
Immigrant Grandparents:
- To children — be more American
- To grandchildren — embrace your native culture

Source: AARP/Business of Aging

Seventy-eight percent of grandparents chose family celebrations as the most important activity with their grandchildren. With the increasing diversity of the population and in families, the desire of older adults to recreate or preserve traditions from their heritage becomes increasingly important.

While grandparents may have raised their first-generation

children to be "more American," they have pivoted in their later years to wanting to teach their grandchildren about their heritage. This manifests itself in spending on books and music, vacations to return to their country of origin, ceremonies and coming of age events for grandchildren, and sharing culinary adventures.

Our research has shown that even American-born grandparents begin to show an interest in their ancestry and share that heritage with grandchildren. Sites like ancestry.com have been built on this trend among older adults.

In interviews with grandmothers, American Girl was cited multiple times as a positive shopping experience with their granddaughters. Grandmothers like the historical aspect of the original line of dolls and books, with an opportunity to learn while playing. They also like the dolls that represent multiple races and ethnicities, with historically accurate stories about their role in history. Girls can also receive *American Girl* magazine. The American Girl stores are designed for multi-generational shopping experiences with activities, workshops, places for parties, and dining.

CASE STUDY:

LEGG MASON ON FUNDING EDUCATION

LEGG MASON
GLOBAL ASSET MANAGEMENT
Legg Mason is an American-based global investment management firm founded in 1899. They are the twentieth largest investment manager in the world serving 6 continents, with more than $700 billion in assets under management.

In 2013, Legg Mason chose to refine its current 529 college savings program to educate grandparents on this method of investment, and to assist grandparents with investing in their grandchildren's education. They launched a research study to understand grandparents, their investments, their role in their grandchildren's lives, and their desire to leave a legacy.

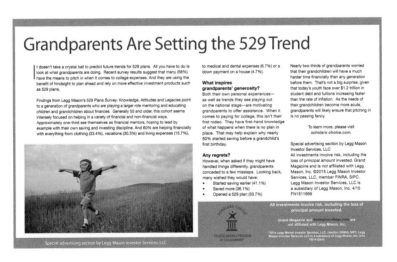

In its recent study Legg Mason learned more about where grandparents are putting their money and their time, and how they value education:

- Forty-seven percent said they help because "my family needs financial assistance" and "I have the financial means."

- They are helping in non-financial ways: 42 percent day-care/babysitting; 39 percent entertainment; helping with homework or tutoring 27 percent.

- It is most important to grandparents to pass down values – the values of the family and the importance of education.

- Four in ten grandparents are currently saving or investing to help with their grandchildren's college expenses and have a 529 Plan.

- Grandparents with less formal education want to help their grandchildren achieve more success than they did themselves.

Legacy

Grandparents of every generation care deeply about their legacy. It is a theme that appeals to Bernbach's "Unchanging Man." Providing an education is a value that resonates across every segment of the grandparent population. Boomers do not place high importance on leaving a tangible inheritance for the next generation, which is a huge change from previous generations who scrimped and saved to make sure they left something to their children. Boomers place a higher value on helping financially when children and grandchildren need help, and on creating experiences with their family while they are alive.

Sharing and teaching values are a recurring theme throughout our research and that of the other studies we have cited as well. The values ranked the highest by today's grandparents are honesty, good behavior, self-sufficiency, higher education, and health habits.

Figure 39

Sharing values

Values grandparents rank highest:		Passing down to grandchildren:	
Honesty	88%	Character	88%
Good behavior	82%	Voting	73%
Self sufficiency	70%	Life Skills	70%
Higher education	69%	Family Ties	67%
Health habits	68%	Volunteering	49%
		Civic Engagement	49%

Source: MetLife Mature Market Institute

They hope to pass down these virtues: voting, volunteering, civic engagement, character, life skills, and family ties.

More telling is how grandparents want their grandchildren to view their legacy.

Figure 40

How grandparents want grandchildren to see their legacy

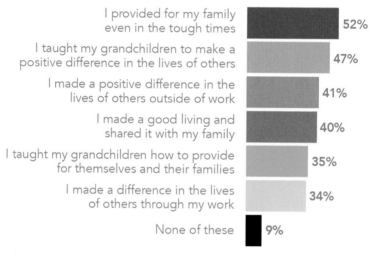

I provided for my family even in the tough times	52%
I taught my grandchildren to make a positive difference in the lives of others	47%
I made a positive difference in the lives of others outside of work	41%
I made a good living and shared it with my family	40%
I taught my grandchildren how to provide for themselves and their families	35%
I made a difference in the lives of others through my work	34%
None of these	9%

Source: MetLife Mature Market Institute and Generations United

Perhaps driven by the recession, more than 50 percent said, "I provided for my family even in the tough times."

In an Encore.org and MetLife Foundation survey, Boomers were asked to envision their later life. Thirty-three percent want to work as long as possible, to cover their expenses and healthcare; 31 percent see it as the beginning of a new chapter where they are active and involved, and helping others. Only 14 percent saw it as a time to take a well-deserved rest and pursue leisure activities. Fully 70 percent want to have made a difference in the world. Let's make that the legacy of the Boomer generation.

Afterword

Recently I read a story by Marc Freedman in *The New York Times*. Marc is always provocative and this story ignited my thinking about the role of grandparents. In the article Marc says that the person who will live to be 150 years old is alive today. He challenged us to think about what we would do with those extra years of our lives:

"In the early decades of the 21st century, we are pushing, rapidly, to extend our lives. But we're paying scant attention to how we should make the most of that additional time. Where are the innovations designed to make these bonus decades actually worth living? Aside from the mind-boggling prospect of saving for 50- or 75-year retirements, how do we make these new chapters both fulfilling for individuals and sustainable for society?"

"Life extension without social innovation is a recipe for dystopian disaster – what one critic characterizes as 'the coming death shortage,' invoking images not only of endless (and unaffordable) retirements but of a society loaded down by a population explosion of the idle old."

My grandmother lived to a wonderful 98 years old. I have always imagined that my life would be long if my lifestyle choices were moderate.

As a grandmother my thoughts immediately went to Gabriel and Henry, my sweet grandsons. Should they live into their 100s how should I counsel them? Is college at 18 important? Should they see the world first, before deciding what to do with the many years ahead of them? Does it make more sense to start a career in your thirties and have a family in your forties? Will biology catch up so that women have expanded childbearing years? How old will Gabriel and Henry be when they become grandfathers?

This is an expansion of possibilities for the middle years of life – truly "life reimagined" as AARP advertises! As an entrepreneur I can envision a career that spans 10 to 15 years, followed by education and perhaps travel; then the launch of a new career that is focused on a passion. Then the later years are focused on family, social entrepreneurship, and volunteering.

Just as we are today rethinking retirement age, the new age of retirement would be very old indeed. We have to fund this extended life span. This will certainly affect the way we live. Today we are talking about three-generation living; what about four or five generations? What will the role of grandparents and great grandparents be? Will elders fill the roles of educators as Margaret Mead suggested? Certainly the world will have to become intergenerationally focused.

Let us not be naïve. There are ethical issues. Just because we can live that long, should we? What would the quality of life be like? Certainly more years in assisted living or skilled nursing care is not the goal. More years will require a greater sense of purpose. And what about planning? Financial products will need to evolve. Will we feel the same way about home ownership and staying in one place? What about the transportation needs of an intergenerational world?

Government at every level would be forced to create real aging policy. Perhaps the White House Council on Aging would be a permanent fixture rather than a periodic meeting during a lame duck term. Cities would have to become more livable for a range of ages. States would require resources for education and infrastructure.

So I circle back. If we know this is our future, and we are currently experiencing the largest population of older adults in the history of the world, what are we waiting for? We need to begin now to think about those "encore" years. The products and services need to begin to evolve. We need to have conversations about the ethical issues of aging and what rights we have when our quality of life is severely diminished. Policy must catch up with the reality of an aging population. Who will lead this country of elders, creating a path for that 150-year-old person to walk down?

As a grandmother, I am going to open my mind to the possibility and help my grandsons understand their opportunities and choices in a world of encore years.

Acknowledgements

This book is one stop on the path of helping businesses see older people in new ways, and to understand their importance not just to our economy, but also to the social fiber of our world. I have been blessed to learn from the smartest people in the aging field. First was Ken Dychtwald and the team at Age Wave Impact, who set me on this course. There I met Chuck Hurst and Scott Adams, two of the smartest research guys I know, and with whom I still work whenever I can. They taught me to require good research and insights, and to know them when I see them. At J Walter Thompson, I got to know the brilliant David Wolfe who changed my thinking about marketing to older adults. I joined "The Society" – his group of smart friends, dedicated to solving the problems of an aging population. Without this band of people, I never would have written a book. As I struck out on my own, I met Mary Furlong, a force of nature in this space. She is a friend and colleague. Her energy, networking skills, and support are unparalleled. I give my thanks and appreciation to each of you for all that you do.

Then there's my merry little team who work with me day-to-day. Thank you to Richard Schwartz for his time, sense of humor, and gentle prodding. He is the best Jewish mother a girl could have. And also to the team of Bruce and Jim at Rubin Cordaro who made the data in this book easy to read, and make me look good, often under tight deadlines. Patrick Mercier, a brilliant digital guy, who because he married my daughter has become my go-to guy for every web site issue and email question. I thank him for that . . . oh, and for my beautiful grandsons! Speaking of *GRAND,* Christine and Jonathan have offered friendship and the *GRAND* platform as my living lab. Finally, I must express my appreciation to the team at Paramount Market Publishing, Doris Walsh, Jim Madden, and Anne Kilgore for helping me see this through to the end. You are wonderful!

My family is the source of my energy, creativity and strength. Most of them are flung across the Midwest, Florida, and New Mexico. They aren't quite sure what I do, but they always support me! Dwain, Ashley, and Kate, we've always been a tight little team. I love how our tribe keeps growing! You are generous in spirit and make every day a better day for me. I love you guys and thank you.

Index

About the Author

Lori Bitter provides strategic consulting, research and development for companies seeking to engage with mature consumers at The Business of Aging. She also serves as publisher of *GRAND Magazine* – the digital magazine for grandparents.

Lori is the former president of Continuum Crew and Crew Media, owner of Eons.com. She was president of J. Walter Thompson's Boomer division, JWT BOOM, the nation's leading mature market advertising and marketing company and led that firm's annual Boomer marketing event for five years. Prior to that she led client service for Age Wave Impact. Lori has more than 30 years of advertising, public relations and strategic planning experience.

A contributor to five books on aging consumers and a leader in research on topics relevant to the senior and Boomer population, Lori has been featured in American Marketing Association's blog, *AARP Magazine,* the *Los Angeles Times, Forbes* magazine and on CNBC. She was named to *Entrepreneur Magazine*'s 100 to Watch List. Lori holds a MS in Advertising, and is a former Associate Professor of Advertising and Public Relations. She serves on the Leadership Council of the College of Media for the University of Illinois.

A sought-after speaker, Lori has presented research, trends and analysis about mature consumers and the longevity marketplace to more than 200 conferences and events in the United States, the United Kingdom and Europe. These include: Booz Allen (UK), Consumer Electronics Show – Silvers Summit, Educational Travel Conference (ETC), American Advertising Federation (AAF), Healthcare Unbound, National Retail Federation, Outdoor Industry Association (OIA), National Association of Recording Merchandisers (NARM), Marketing to Women Conference (M2W), White House Council on Aging Meetings, National Association of Home Builders (NAHB), Gerontological Society of America (GSA), American Society on Aging (ASA), What's Next Boomer Summit, Assisted Living Federation of America (ALFA), AARP, International Mature Market Network (IMMN), AgeTek, California Assisted Living Association (CALA), Leading Age, United Methodist Church Foundation, and many similar events.

She has served as a judge and panelist for numerous award and business competitions, including the American Advertising Federation (AAF) and the North American Effie awards.

Lori lives in San Francisco, close to her grandsons, and enjoys traveling with them whenever she can.